Praise for *Barbara Anderson Uncensored*

Praise by **Mariuca Rofick**, an artist, former Jehovah's Witness and one of the subjects of the book *Mariuca & Marilyn, Saying Good-Bye to Mama's Club.*

Nothing short of awe-inspiring – Mariuca Rofick

Barbara is a tireless warrior whose story is as unique as it is awe-inspiring. Her valor in the face of an epic David vs Goliath battle to protect children against the policies of an international organization demonstrates how the efforts of one person, who stands up for right, truly can effect change.

Praise by *Lee Elder*, a former JW elder and founder and manager of the well-researched website on Watchtower blood transfusion policy, ajwrb.org.

I found myself spellbound by Barbara's story – Lee Elder

My first introduction to Barbara came through her interview on NBC's Dateline in 2002. (https://vimeo.com/160789542) We occasionally exchanged emails over the years, but it would be more than a decade before I met Barbara and her husband Joe. While I've known of her tireless advocacy for JW children who have been sexually abused, the details of her story remained mostly unknown to me.

Having had the opportunity to read an advance copy of her story, I found myself spellbound by her account, in much the same way as when I first read "Crisis of Conscience" by Ray Franz. Here you will find a unique perspective on how things work at Watchtower headquarters. Her time at Bethel as a researcher yielded some real nuggets regarding the history of the Watchtower that were previously unknown, and expose how the Watchtower whitewashes its history.

Barbara reveals the deep divisions that existed between the Writing and Service Departments in the 1990's, and how hard liners like Ted Jaracz, and progressives like Lloyd Barry fought to influence Watchtower policy on child abuse. Eventually Barbara managed to escape suffocating in that intellectual wasteland, and summoned the courage to blow the whistle on the Watchtower's child sexual abuse coverup. Her story is a compelling one which I thoroughly enjoyed.

Praise by *Joanna Foreman*, Author of *The Know-it-all Girl Grows Up* and *Riverwalk Chameleon*, and a former Jehovah's Witness.

"While my head tells me that I am an historian, my heart tells me that I am an activist." ~ Barbara Anderson

Imagine a female researcher and writer in the 1980's, an assistant to men in high-ranking positions in a century-old religious organization—the Watchtower Society of Jehovah's Witnesses. An organization that was run by males—men with secrets intentionally kept from the society's loyal followers.

While working with those men in the Writing Department at the World Headquarters in Brooklyn, New York, Barbara Anderson investigated Watchtower's early history. With access to the archives, she blew the dust off of boxes that had long ago been placed in cabinets and forgotten. Her discoveries proved that her religion, which touted itself as *The Truth,* had both hidden and misrepresented *real* truth for years. When she learned of the rampant child sex abuse which had been kept tucked away, she immediately called for change.

However, the organization's hierarchy refused to alter their misleading tactics. Barbara withdrew from the religion, making her reasons clear. Her role changed from a researcher and writer to an activist and historian. Her contributions have earned her worldwide acclaim as an advocate for the rights of children and molestation victims.

I highly recommend reading *Barbara Anderson, Uncensored.* It is a candid narrative of a worldwide religion, one that most people have seen as harmless until now. Ms. Anderson also offers a workable plan of action for change.

Praise by **Lee Marsh,** a former victim of child sexual abuse and the President of Advocates for Awareness of Watchtower Abuses (aawa.co).

Barbara's unique story shines a beacon of hope for victims of child molestation – Lee Marsh

I was introduced to Barbara Anderson when she started posting on an ex-Jehovah's Witness website, sharing information about the vast number of JW children that were and are being sexually abused within JW congregations worldwide.

Her desire to shed light on this heinous crime committed on thousands of innocent children inspired me and other survivors to come out and tell our stories. And for that, I will always be grateful.

Barbara's unique story shines a beacon of hope for victims of child molestation and how Watchtower unduly influences its members to not report abuses to the proper authorities. If anyone can expose Watchtower's deference to protecting its money-making organization over the rights of the children, Barbara is uniquely qualified to do the job.

Praise by *Frances Peters*, a Certified Academic/Counselor and the spokesperson for the Open Minds Foundation in the Netherlands.

This eye-opening book will also give readers a rare peek behind the scenes of how policies and beliefs are formed at the world headquarters for JWs – Frances Peters

Barbara Anderson's interview on Dateline in 2002, about the pervasiveness of child molestation among Jehovah's Witnesses, was life changing for many JWs. My *defining* moment came a few months after the interview, when I watched a documentary, *"Suffer the little children."* It aired on BBC's television program Panorama and the show was based on Barbara's research on JW paedophilia.

As a born-and-raised JW and mother of two, the show hit me hard. I knew she was telling the truth. Only someone with integrity could do what she did, while sacrificing so much. Several local child abuse cases that I personally knew about only confirmed the truthfulness of her story.

Before the show, I believed these child abuse cases were a local problem. Now I knew that Watchtower's policy on how to handle child molestation issues was the problem and that made the organization unsafe. So, I decided to leave.

Reading Barbara's story gifted me with additional insights into the challenges she faced early in her discovery process. I have a huge respect for her courage and patience in handling this situation. This unique book, about a woman who has changed so many lives, will also give readers a rare peek behind the scenes of how policies and beliefs are formed at the world headquarters for JWs.

Praise by *Mark J. O'Donnell*, a writer, researcher and advocate for child protection and the elimination of undue influence.

Something went terribly wrong and within ten years, Barbara would uncover a conflict that would derail her plans, and change her life forever – Mark O'Donnell

In 1982, Barbara Anderson arrived in Brooklyn, New York, filled with energy, optimism and faith. The Jehovah's Witness religion was in the midst of rapid global expansion. Barbara had a front row seat, a permanent place inside the epicenter of an organization boasting new peaks in membership every month.

For JWs at that time, the end of the corrupt world was near, the future was bright, and there was no better place to be than the Brooklyn Bethel Headquarters. But something went terribly wrong. Within 10 years, Barbara would uncover a conflict that would derail her plans, and change her life forever.

The first time I read Barbara Anderson's story, the details, names and places jumped out at me with factual accuracy and candor. I felt her pain, struggling to navigate the hurdles she faced as a woman in a male-dominated organization. Her research skills, knowledge, and abilities propelled her on to a collision course with the religion she had dedicated her life to.

Barbara's story is one of integrity and valor. As a wife, mother, and an advocate for children around the globe, Barbara speaks for the thousands of victims of child abuse whose voices have been silenced. She speaks for the children who have been needlessly placed in harm's way. At one time we were all children who needed protection, which is why Barbara's story speaks to every one of us.

It is my honor to highly recommend this book, and the ongoing efforts of Barbara and her associates to bring about the reform needed to keep our children safe.

Barbara Anderson *Uncensored*
Eyewitness To Deceit

Discoveries of a Former Jehovah's Witness Insider

Barbara Anderson
with
Richard E. Kelly

Parker Ridge Publishing Tucson, Arizona

Readers may contact the publisher at:
parkerridgepubs@gmail.com

This edition was prepared for publishing by
Ghost River Images
5350 East Fourth Street
Tucson, Arizona 85711
www.ghostriverimages.com

Cover art by Carl Wilson
www.carlwilsonart.com

ISBN 978-0-9795094-8-3

Library of Congress Control Number: 2018941141

Printed in the United States of America
April 2018

Contents

Dedication

This book is dedicated to the thousands of children who were sexually molested while growing up as Jehovah's Witnesses.

~ Barbara Anderson

~~~

"When a Jehovah's Witness child is sexually abused by a member of their congregation, it is a terrifying thing for the child to consider reporting the offender to a trusted adult. The terror is exacerbated when the child learns he or she must also report this abuse to a "judicial committee" of three male elders–requiring the child to endure an onslaught of probing, intrusive questions.

The child's protective autonomic nervous-system response (to fight, to flee, or to freeze) will kick in to help them cope with this secondary abuse. Abused children realize they cannot "fight" back in this judicial meeting and they are not allowed to "flee" the room. The only response left is for the nervous system to have them "freeze" – shut down, withdraw internally, or dissociate. Of course there are rarely, if ever, any other witnesses to a molestation who can step up and fill in the details of the crime for the child.

Because JW elders are required to apply a Bible verse saying that "two witnesses" to a crime are required to substantiate any allegations, the pedophile often escapes any consequences and resumes their activities in the congregation.

The JW elders conducting the interrogation of the sexually abused child are not professionally trained to handle such situations and invariably have no comprehension of the harm they are doing to an already abused and suffering child."

~ Bonnie Zieman, M.Ed., psychotherapist

(More information is available on pages 42-43 on the impact of sexual abuse on JW children)

11

Preface

Why Barbara Anderson's Story is so Important

By Richard E. "Dick" Kelly

Today Barbara Anderson is an unstoppable advocate for the protection of children and an outspoken critic of the Watchtower Society's doctrines and policies that protect sexual predators and unduly influence Jehovah's Witnesses to believe that their policies are Bible-based and inspired from God. She is also an expert on Watchtower's history and, for me, a modern-day hero.

But the advocacy piece of Barbara's story is a recent phenomena, not yet 20 years old. For most of her adult life, she was a true-believing, walk-the-talk member of a cult, which masquerades as God's chosen people. A psuedo-religious group that excels at disguising their psychological-manipulating skills, brainwashing if you will, to attract and keep people like Barbara as members.

As a JW, Barbara was cloned with *the new personality* Watchtower had imposed upon her, as opposed to the authentic identity she so proudly wears today. This juxtaposition provides the ingredients for a great story, which you're about to read.

However, for many of you unfamiliar with how easily the mind can be controlled by predators or predatory groups, you may wonder why it took Barbara so long to wake up to the reality that she was in a manipulative high-control group. So I am grateful for the enlightening commentary of Bonnie Zieman and Jon Atack in

13

this book. They will report behind the scenes what was going on in Barbara's high-control world and her subsequent escape from a physical and psychological point of view. Bonnie and Jon excel at articulating the dynamics of coercive control.

While I believe their commentary is critical to the success of this story, it could be distracting when you read Barbara's condensed story for the first time. For that reason, I have created smaller font-sized breaks in the story to alert you where I have asked Bonnie and Jon to share their insights, although their actual comments are found in the commentary (pages 53-64). For many, you may want to skip past these breaks, and read them and the subsequent comments on your second read of Barbara's story.

About six years ago, Barbara and I talked about collaborating to write and tell her incredible story. This would have been a mammoth project, at least for me, if we could have pulled it off. There was so much to tell. While I accumulated hundreds of documents and saved a box load of notes from our long conversations, her story sat dormant for several years.

In 2017, while reading chapter 32—*Barbara Anderson's Discoveries*—from Poul Bregninge's *Judgment Day Must Wait*, a light bulb went off in my head. I decided then and there that I must find a way to tell her story now! Even if it was only a condensed version, her story is too compelling *not* to tell. So I contacted Barbara and we started to work on the short teaser-like story you are about to read.

Barbara and I are also grateful for a handful of people, especially Bonnie Zieman, who read several drafts of this story and provided excellent advice. You will find their reviews of the book in the introduction and their bios in the sections, "Significant Help From My Friends" on pages 87-94.

Barbara has assured me that this book will not be the last written about her life and what she has learned about Watchtower and its sordid history. She is particularly passionate about telling the life story of Maria Russell (the founder's wife), but first things first.

You should also know that Barbara showcases an impressive library of stories on her website, http://watchtowerdocuments.

org/document-library/. During the course of the read, she will refer you to this library where additional stories and anecdotal information can be found.

Like many cult-like groups, Watchtower uses *loaded language* to rally members to their unique cause, utilizing language which is foreign to most non-JWs. For this reason we have provided a glossary of terms and words that JWs use. You can find this on pages 77-80.

This book has been made possible because of a grant/gift from the Open Minds Foundation at https://www.openmindsfounda-tion.org/.

Making This Book Accessible to Non-Jehovah's Witnesses

Reading Barbara's story without a basic understanding of certain specialized names, terms and practices—*Armageddon, elders, shunning, Bethel, apostate, the two-witness rule* and the legal differences between *Watchtower-Jehovah's Witnesses* and *JW.ORG*—could make reading this book a challenge.

While most people know the dictionary meanings of these terms and words, we want you to understand the way JW.ORG uses them, which is to threaten, instill fear, evoke loyalty and exercise control. To that end, we have provided the following explanations, which we hope will add clarity for non-JW readers:

Armageddon

Fear of God's "*Battle of Armageddon*" is instilled into every JW. Even books for children contain images of God's army of angels annihilating the "*wicked*" (everyone not a JW) at this "*end-of-the-world*" apocalypse. JW publications often contain images of Armageddon's aftermath, showing non-believing families piled lifeless upon each other, in obscene portrayals of the ultimate holocaust. While in the forefront of the same image loyal, surviving JWs raise their arms in gratitude that Jehovah has fulfilled his promise to destroy all wickedness and restore an earthly paradise – just for them.

With the threat of destruction at Armageddon mentioned repeatedly in JW publications and sermons, JWs are always on guard against any demonstration of *"sin"*, *"disobedience"*, *"worldliness"*, or *"independent thinking"*. To stray from the teachings and practices of the Watchtower will seal one's fate: a merciless, violent, eternal death by Jehovah and his avenging angels at the Battle of Armageddon. Armageddon is used as a fundamental control mechanism, which is an ever-hovering threat to ensure the obedience and loyalty of their members.

Bethel

JWs cleverly name their world headquarters "Bethel" (meaning *"house of God"* in Hebrew). For the average JW, Bethel is as holy as the Vatican for Catholics. While JWs do not have a Pope, they have 7 to 10 *"anointed"* men living in this house of God who decide upon all the beliefs, policies and practices this group must follow. To be invited to *"serve"* (volunteer to work in the office, printing, cleaning or cooking work) at Bethel (which across two centuries has been a profit-making printing and real-estate conglomerate) is considered one of the most significant *"privileges"* a JW can have.

Bethel is, they claim, where Jehovah reveals *"new truths"* to his *"chosen representatives"* by having his *"holy spirit"* descend upon the minds and hearts of the male-only members of the Governing Body. Rank-and-file members are encouraged to use their vacations and vacation pay to visit Bethel—and while it is never named as a required pilgrimage for every JW—it definitely holds that level of importance for them. To be invited to work in Bethel, and especially to be invited to work with or for the divinely-inspired *"Governing Body"* or those who minister to them and manage the operations, is considered a high honor.

Unfortunately, Watchtower demonstrates little duty-of-care to people who have sacrificed normal lives to work at Bethel. Aged members receive no pension after decades of loyal service. Many who have *"served"* in these positions and then leave, recount their high expectations about what they would experience when they entered Bethel and how disappointed they became as those expectations were dashed. Bethel, they discovered, holds many unsavory secrets.

Elders

In each congregation around the world, elders are appointed to lead and apply Watchtower principles and practices to the members. Elders also judge and discipline errant members. There is no special training to become an elder—it is determined by experience in the organization, knowledge of the JW publications and Watchtower's version of the Bible, and their level of devotion, which must be validated by a special representative from Watchtower's headquarters.

Elders are assigned the task of interpreting, explaining and enforcing all dogma, practices and expected behaviors of the members. JWs are trained from childhood to look up to elders and not to question their decisions or how they discipline fellow members, any more than they would question the edicts that emanate from the governing body members at the world headquarters known as Bethel.

Each congregation has several male-only elders. They are assigned different roles, which are required to maintain function of the congregation. But there is not one in particular who calls himself the minister or pastor of the group. Male members of each congregation are encouraged to aspire to be an elder.

It is the elders of a congregation who administer the *judicial hearings* that are called to determine what will be done about any reports of wrongdoing within the JW community. The elders make decisions about whether or not behaviors qualify as sexual abuse, whether illegal activities will be reported to the authorities and whether a congregant will receive the ultimate punishment—being banished from the congregation and shunned by all the remaining members.

The power that these unschooled men are given over people's lives would be unthinkable in secular society. Yet, elders can require members to stop all association with family members

19

who are deemed to have disobeyed Watchtower's rules. In fact, it is possible for an elder who works all day cleaning windows to exercise dominion over the lives of the loyal congregants.

Apostate

JWs are taught to assume that if a person leaves the group it is because they are engaged in pagan or demonic activities. The word *apostate* is used to stigmatize JW defectors and to make loyal members terrified to listen to anything a so-called apostate has to say, as it could infect them to demon-inspired thoughts. The term has become so loaded by JW.ORG that most JWs quake when they hear it–and worse yet–run in terror if they ever come close to an apostate.

Watchtower is not simply interested in name-calling with their use of the term apostate. It is a conscious effort to demonize the one who leaves, and keep faithful JWs afraid to read outside material (*it could be written by an apostate!*), afraid to speak to anyone who has left the organization (*they could be an apostate and infect me with pagan ideas!*), and terrified to do anything that would have the elders put them in this vile category (*if I do this I could be disfellowshipped and called an apostate!*). The use of this term is another one of Watchtower's cunning methods of control.

Shunning

Watchtower mandates shunning or ostracism to control its members. Anyone who leaves the organization, even close family members, must be totally shunned. To be willing and able to shun defectors or independent thinkers is treated as a demonstration of one's ultimate loyalty to Watchtower's God, Jehovah. When confronted by the general public about this inhumane policy of shunning, Witness officials and the rank and file often claim that JWs do not shun. They say that it is the person leaving the organization who is shunning Jehovah and His people. But, their own publications disprove this false claim.

Currently, Watchtower does not suffer any legal consequences for its mandated shunning policy. And yet, this practice tears families apart and even ruptures crucial family ties between parents and minor children. This adversely affects a person's long-term well-being and also causes people who cannot cope with such inhumanity to commit suicide–all with impunity by Watchtower.

The Two-Witness Rule

Jehovah's Witnesses require two eyewitnesses to a molestation of a child before a child is believed. In other words, if a child reports to the congregation elders that he or she was sexually abused, the child is not believed unless there is another eyewitness, who saw and will confirm the molestation accusation.

Jehovah's Witnesses, Watchtower and JW.ORG

It is the name of the corporation and the legal entity, *Watchtower*, to which we will refer in this book.

In 1879, the name Watchtower began to be associated with a relatively unknown group, the Bible Students, identified since 1931 as Jehovah's Witnesses. It was in July 1879 when ZION'S WATCH TOWER magazine was first published by the group. The name of that magazine today is simply *The Watchtower.*

In addition, this group's first corporation, known today as WATCH TOWER Bible and Tract Society of Pennsylvania, was created in 1884. The Bible Students' second corporation was created in 1909. In 1937, it changed its name to Watchtower Bible and Tract Society, adding 'of New York, Inc.' in 1956.

In 2012, JW.ORG became Watchtower's official website and the online source of information about the beliefs and activities of Jehovah's Witnesses. The website is published and maintained by Watchtower Bible and Tract Society of New York, Inc., which is just one of Watchtower's many corporations.

(A Glossary of all the unique and loaded language used by Jehovah's Witnesses can be found on pages 77-80.)

Barbara Anderson *Uncensored*

Eyewitness To Deceit

Discoveries of a Former Jehovah's Witness Insider
Written by Barbara Anderson with Richard E. Kelly

"They were men convicted of child sexual molestation, incarcerated in prisons across the US, and converted after studying the Bible with Jehovah's Witness elders, who were active in the JW "prison ministry." These were the men "known" in the "community" mentioned in the letter. After release from prison and baptism, many of them went on to molest the children of the divorced JW women they married." – From page 38

A Life Altering Choice

I was born in Long Island, NY, in 1940 to Polish Catholic parents. Dad and Mom never went to church except on Easter. That stopped after my confirmation at age 11, when they decided after a visit by a local priest that the church was more about making money than helping people. I stopped going to church when I was 12, after learning that two of my Catholic girl friends had just been molested by a priest.

For the next two years in my bedroom at night, I was secretly reading and trying to understand the Bible. By doing so, I hoped to ward off my insecurity and fears. Those were the atomic bomb years in the 1950s when during school drills we kids had to hunker down and squeeze under our desks to be prepared for a bomb attack.

My fears were kindled early from watching newsreels of World War II, when my grandma took me to the movies on Saturday afternoon. Our relatives lived in Poland, so these film clips were personal. Watching children desperately trapped behind the barbed wire of concentration camps was especially disturbing for me.

In 1953, while I was visiting at the home of one of my school chums, the doorbell rang. I opened the door and explained that my friend's mother was not available. That didn't bother the lady and she started using her Bible to tell me about a new world to come *without war*, which really grabbed my attention. When the lady asked if she could come to my home and *study the Bible* with me, I was all in.

I was a discontented 13-year old, with zero knowledge of the Bible, so it was easy for the lady to spin scripture to support her claim for a future world without war. When I was baptized in 1954, I just narrowed my opportunities to make choices for the next 43 years, because I joined one of the most aggressive, controversial religions, Jehovah's Witnesses (JWs), and it became the center of my life.

I'd like to stop here, as most of you are probably thinking: How could I at 13 years of age make such a significant decision like that? What was I thinking? So I asked a therapist and writer, Bonnie Zieman, M.Ed., to explain how I was manipulated. She explains on pages 53-54, #1

At 19, I married Joe Anderson, one of the kindest persons I have ever known. Still is. We met the year before when he worked at *Bethel,* the world headquarters for JWs. Joe operated one of the printing presses there from 1956 - 1959.

At 18, Joe's mother and I attended the same congregation in Long Island and she invited several single girls to the house for a Saturday afternoon get-together to meet her son and several of his Bethel buddies. To get the party going and to try to match Joe and me up, she played a tango record on the record machine. Joe asked each of us girls to dance with him, but no one shared his ballroom dancing skills except me. I was the only one who could tango, and we've been tangoing ever since. In this case, "momma knew best" because the attraction was immediate.

After getting married, Joe and I *pioneered* (100 hours a month in the *door-to-door ministry*) until I learned I was pregnant. Our son, Lance, was born September 1961.

But that did not stop us, as Joe held a position of authority in every *congregation* we belonged to – most of the time the *presiding overseer*. Joe also spent over 25 years in the full-time volunteer *pioneer* ministry. In the early years of our marriage, we supported our family through part-time work. I worked in accounting and for a physician. Joe learned how to be a plumber in the building construction trades from a JW he had studied with and converted.

Over the years we converted more than 80 people to our faith, because we were able to convince them of a better world to come; a world without war and fear. At the time we put our trust in Watchtower's theology, as they appeared to have Biblical answers to age-old questions about life, death and how to please God.

Although the 1975 date set by JWs for the Apocalypse (*Armageddon*) came and went—a failed prophecy—Joe and I were not deterred. Joe had lived and worked at Bethel, so he knew men like Fred Franz could be eccentric and were not always correct with their predictions. For me, I had personally invested 21 years of my life in the religion and was not about to throw in the towel.

Sounds crazy, doesn't it? But that's how the brain can be fooled by a cult-like group. To help you understand how this works, I've asked a cult expert and writer, Jon Atack, to explain how even the most rational of people can be tricked, as he does on pages 54-55, #2

Volunteer Work

In 1982 Watchtower invited Joe and me to become volunteer staff members at their headquarters—Bethel—in Brooklyn Heights, NY. The year before, our 19-year-old son, Lance, was invited to work at Bethel and operated one of their many high-speed printing presses, which annually turned out millions of pieces of literature.

My husband was the reason we were invited to Bethel. When visiting our son in March 1982, Joe was talking to one of the factory supervisors. When he found out Joe was a plumber, he started the ball rolling so we could come work at Bethel.

Sometime later, we found out why Bethel officials were eager to recruit plumbers like Joe. Negotiations were underway to purchase a dilapidated factory with over a million square feet near the East River. In addition, the rundown 12-story Bossert Hotel was secretly being considered for purchase, as were 15 additional buildings near Bethel. The intent was to use these buildings to house future Bethelites and to expand shipping capacity. Within the next 15 years, Watchtower would own nearly 20 residential buildings, all of them renovated with free JW labor and tax exempt.

Since Brooklyn Heights was deemed an historic district, renovated buildings had to meet specific requirements. One of my jobs at Bethel was to research historical and architectural details to meet those requirements, as I had worked for the last 5 years for a building contractor as the manager and bookkeeper for two of the businesses the contractor owned.

One afternoon, while working as the secretary for an architect designing a 30-story staff residence building for Bethelites, I stood waiting for an elevator in the office building where I worked. John

("Jack") Barr, a Governing Body member, joined me and while we patiently waited for a slow-moving elevator, he asked what I was doing. I told him that our group was rushing to complete an Environmental Impact Statement. The data in the EIS document would be used by the City of New York to consider our request for a zoning change at a location where Watchtower wanted to build the 30-story building. There was significant community opposition to our requested waterfront site, which was located on the Brooklyn side of the East River and would block the famous view of the lower Manhattan Wall Street area.

I'll never forget Jack saying, "We've set aside fifty million dollars for this project, and it's amazing to see how the money we have in the bank never decreases." Then he added, "Jehovah always provides!" All the while gesturing with his right hand to draw an imaginary horizontal line from left to right indicating the money stays constant. However, Jehovah did not provide approval for the zoning change. The residence building was eventually built a few blocks inland, next to our factories, but it was far from what was considered as an ideal location.

While writing this story, I remembered another very important experience I had while working in the Engineering Dept. If you are interested in reading this story, please visit my website at http://watchtowerdocuments.org/document-library/.

After 6 years in the engineering department, and due to my proven research skills, I was transferred to the Writing Department in 1989. The work I did was unique for a woman, an aberration, as Watchtower's organizational structure is totally male dominated.

A women's role as a JW and a Bethelite is to be submissive "spiritually" to her husband and Watchtower's male-only leadership, which I was. But the job I was assigned to do gave me a significant amount of freedom to make decisions without asking permission from anyone. I could come and go as I pleased, and in spite of females being at the bottom of the pecking order in the organization, I was never treated as an inferior, especially by my husband and the men I worked for.

Surprising Discoveries

While I worked in the Writing Department, my supervisor was senior staff writer Karl Adams. He was writing the history of JWs in what would become *Jehovah's Witnesses Proclaimers of God's Kingdom*, a 750-page book published in 1993. Karl gave me questions that he wanted researched about Watchtower's early history and I had permission from the *Governing Body* members of JWs to do research in any part of the huge complex of offices. I learned a great deal as I discovered archival material that had long ago been placed in cabinets and forgotten.

One thing I discovered was that William H. Conley, a banker, *not* Charles Taze Russell, (as Watchtower had reported to members for over 100 years) was the first president of the Watch Tower Association formed in 1881. Russell's father, Joseph, was vice president and Charles secretary-treasurer. The appointment was based on purchases of $10 shares. This was all new to the senior management of the Watchtower organization, although Karl decided to share only a part of this information with the rank-and-file Jehovah's Witness.

When I first read this early history about Watchtower, I had to read it a second time, albeit very slowly as my heart raced with excitement. I couldn't believe my eyes; a moment in time I will never forget. It never occurred to me that it could be a cover-up, as this information was gleaned from documents squeezed into storage boxes mothballed for years.

At one time, while researching another question for Karl, I read the divorce trial cross-examination transcript of Charles Russell. I was not allowed to read the transcript of Maria Russell's cross-examination, and I assumed that was because I would need special training to understand court papers. But years later, my curiosity got the best of me, and I read it. This turned out to be a shocker for me as Maria's problems with Russell were totally misrepresented to JWs in Watchtower literature.

I was not allowed to read Maria's testimony. Today, I would not tolerate something like this, as I question everything, especially when it comes to gender equality. But cult dynamics and undue influence were at play at this time of my life, as Jon Atack will explain on pages 55-56, #3.

During another assignment Karl gave me, I examined what led up to indictments of President Rutherford for obstructing enlistment of military service for American citizens during WW I. When he learned the United States government objected to 7 pages in *The Finished Mystery*, he cut those pages out of all the copies. When he found out that distribution of the books was in violation of the Espionage Act, Rutherford directed distribution to be suspended. Despite all such efforts, Rutherford was sentenced to a long term in a federal penitentiary, but he was later released after the end of the war.

Reading Rutherford's words in the trial transcript altered my perspective of him. During the trial, he said he did everything possible to placate the authorities and did not understand why they were dealing so harshly with him. Karl said privately to me how amazed he was to read Rutherford's conciliatory statements. To Karl, it was clear Rutherford compromised his integrity, telling me that his guilt had to be the reason why he vowed, when he came out of prison, to go full speed ahead *to announce the good news of God's Kingdom* no matter how severe the persecution. However, Karl decided to censor any mention of Rutherford's poor judgment.

One thing was plain from my research of Rutherford: He had a knack for stirring up trouble by attacking and baiting religions, the clergy and governments. This would incite acts of retribution, the victims of such being the Bible Students and JWs, with Rutherford claiming it was persecution as fulfilment of Jesus' prophesy and not a result of his provocative rhetoric.

During the two years I assisted Karl, my research revealed many surprises about Watchtower, both good and bad. But the negative discoveries did not, at least not yet, give me a reason to doubt my JW beliefs. As a true believer, it was easier to think that objectionable behavior by Watchtower leaders was just "people junk," not in any way a reflection of the validity of the religion.

I was not ready to believe negative information about Watchtower, as I had been programmed to reject it as a people problem and not Watchtower's, as Bonnie explains on pages 56-57, #4.

My Friend Harry

Among my best memories at Bethel was my friendship with Harry Peloyan, a writer and editor for the *Awake!* Harry was a true believer, but his beliefs were not set in stone and he could change his view if he thought a policy wasn't rational or scriptural. He respected my opinion and women in general, which was not always the case at Bethel. A Harvard graduate, he was by far the smartest man that I had ever met.

As I gained his trust, Harry shared what he believed were two huge problems: child sexual abuse accusations among JWs and Watchtower's lack of response. It was so serious that record keeping, from as far back as 1969, of such conduct by JWs from around the world was being compiled by *the Service Department*; the Department that controls the day-to-day operation and policies of Watchtower's organization.

Seldom, if ever, were these accusations of child sexual abuse reported to the police. Rather, most of the accusations were handled secretly by *judicial committees* with no training in these matters. If victims were unhappy with the results, it mattered little. The abused or family of the abused had to keep quiet—it was to be censured—because reporting this to the authorities would *bring reproach upon Jehovah's organization*.

Jon Atack reports on the control of information and need for secrecy in cults on page 57, #5

The abuse of women by domineering, patriarchal men in the *organization* also bothered Harry. Both of us knew that many JW husbands misused their authority as head of the house. But busy with my work, I buried my worries and concerns, thinking men such as Harry, his supervisor, Lloyd Barry (a *Governing Body member* and head of the Writing Department), had everything under control. They would surely find a way to resolve these problems. It had not yet occurred to me that these problems were systemic with a male-dominated predatory culture.

Watchtower's Clumsy Policies

While working with Harry for 12 months in 1992, I learned how pervasive child sexual abuse was among JWs worldwide. Harry did his best to help victims recover by approving an article "Healing the Wounds of Child Abuse," published in the October 8, 1991 *Awake!* But not everyone was like Harry.

The head of the Service Department, Ted Jaracz, was opposed to helping victims seek mental health counselling. So while Harry and Lloyd Barry tried to mitigate the problem in the Writing Department, Jaracz told his staff and *elders*, who reported to him in the Service Department, "Therapists are the devil's agents." Jaracz's cure-all for victims was "to get over it and read Watchtower publications."

Jon Atack explains why psychologists are a "no-no" for men like Jaracz on pages 57-58, #6

Jaracz was also very influential with most of the old-school, geriatric Governing Body members—a committee of men who managed all of Watchtower's business. Because of Jaracz's argumentation, these men believed that applying Bible examples, rules, and principles would restore one's psychological stability; even if they were suffering from depression. Yes, reading the Bible, going to meetings and in the door-to-door ministry would, somehow, cure whatever ails one.

A Maze of Contradictions Between the Service and Writing Departments

Service Department personnel were giving poor advice to elders, when victims asked for help. But, if a victim talked with personnel in the Writing Department, they were treated compassionately and given up-to-date information about their condition. There was a maze of contradiction between departments with victims being re-victimized with Jaracz's misguided solutions. That is why Lloyd Barry authorized *Awake!* articles to be written about recovery, all based on proven secular science.

By the end of 1991, *elders*, who attended *the Kingdom Ministry Schools* (and in two letters to all the elders in March 1992), were informed: "Professional therapy should not to be condemned as in the past and seeking treatment from professional therapists is a personal decision, although one should use caution."

By the time that March letter was received by the elders, hundreds of letters and phone calls were received by Watchtower related to the October 1991 *Awake!* To victims, the article was a breath of fresh air, but nothing really changed. Within the inner sanctums of the congregations, the dirty secrets continued with pressure put on the victims to remain silent, and not to share negative information with therapists or the police.

Soon, Lloyd Barry authorized another article on the child abuse subject to appear in the April 8, 1992 *Awake!* It was entitled, "I Wept for Joy." This article featured quotes from the hundreds of letters that were received in which victims and their friends and families expressed deep appreciation to the Governing Body members for the articles about healing the wounds of child abuse. While Barry was away, Jaracz tried to stop the press room from printing the April article, but Jack Barr, Barry's assistant, another Governing Body member, overruled him.

Did I Go Too Far?

For the first time at Bethel, I experienced this sick feeling that if Jaracz found out I knew about the child sexual abuse problems and was trying to assist with solutions, he'd set up a kangaroo court and disfellowship me. He had orchestrated it many times over the last 12 years, firing up a paranoid group of weak Governing Body members. I wouldn't be the first accused of not supporting the official position of God's organization, even if the policy was unscriptural or violated human rights.

This was very new and very scary for me. I was unable to connect the dots at the time, although my primal brain was telling me to take flight as Bonnie Zieman explains on pages 58-59, #7.

Long-time writer Bill Cetnar, expressed concern about the blood transfusion policy and was promptly demoted from his Bethel *assignment*. After he left Bethel and spoke about this issue, he was disfellowshipped and shunned. After 5 days of being interrogated and yelled at by 7 different Bethel elders, Nestor Kuilan refused to share conversations he had had with Ray Franz, and was disfellowshipped. Other high-profile JWs who were metaphysically executed were James Penton, Ed Dunlap and ex-Governing Body member, Ray Franz.

My fears were also fanned by Ciro Aulicino, a long-term Bethelite who worked with me in the Writing Department. He told me many scary stories about injustices and high-ranking officials at Bethel, who thought they were above the law.

Ciro believed that Knorr's choice of inviting Ted Jaracz to Bethel as a Governing Body member should have been challenged. In 1956, after serving 5 years as the Australian branch overseer, accusations of misconduct about Jaracz were brought to Knorr's attention. Knorr asked Lloyd Barry, a branch overseer at the time, to investigate. The result was that Barry recommended Jaracz's removal and Knorr did just that and sent Jaracz back to the States and Southern California.

After several months in exile, Knorr wrote Jaracz and said if he would get married, Knorr would put him back in play as a *circuit overseer*. Jaracz knew a JW woman in Victoria, Canada, who for years had been begging him to marry her. So, he headed north, and after they were married, Jaracz was assigned to serve as a circuit overseer and later a *district overseer* in the state of California.

This story about Jaracz could only happen in a secretive group like Watchtower. Without a transparent system of accountability, bad things happen as Jon explains on page 59, #8.

Ciro knew Jaracz did something seriously wrong and suspected sexual misconduct, hearing rumors of child sexual abuse. What Knorr and others knew for sure was that Jaracz would never forgive Barry for recommending his removal. The open disgust that Jaracz and Barry had for each other was known by many at Bethel. Frankly, their dislike for each other was obvious to anyone who worked with them.

Richard Wheelock, the Bethel factory supervisor who recruited my husband Joe as a plumber to Bethel, had committed suicide two years before. He stepped out of the 3rd floor window in the building we lived in. Everyone knew Richard suffered from severe depression after his wife died. While some efforts were made to get him some mental health assistance by a JW doctor, it was too little too late. However, knowledge of this tragic event helped to soften the Governing Body's stance on seeking outside help from mental health experts.

But how long would this last? With someone like Jaracz in an influential position, he could decide to attack my work and advice at any time. It did not help that I was working for Jaracz's detractor, Lloyd Barry. I would wake up in a cold sweat at night, thinking that two hard-core Bethel elders, summoned by Jaracz, could appear in my department any day and demand my loyalty to Watchtower's policies.

I could easily be disfellowshipped and shunned by my family and friends with Jaracz ramrodding my concocted unrighteousness and labeling me *an apostate*. This would nullify all my good work and prevent more good work in the future.

Terminating Bethel Service

So in August of 1992, while I was still a well-respected, contributing writer, Joe and I decided to terminate our stay at Bethel. We would leave at the end of the year. I was the driving force behind that decision, as I deplored Watchtower's lack of desire to address serious child sexual and domestic abuse problems. I was also disgusted by their refusal to assist victims, and I was afraid of Jaracz. But I kept my opinions to myself, only sharing them with my husband.

However, our leaving was not as simple as giving a notice. Karl Adams and his brother, Joel, a Governing Body member, were not happy. They wanted us to stay. We were both valuable hard-working contributors to Watchtower's current success. When I said we were moving back to Tennessee to help my aging parents, Joel responded by saying that if we stayed, Watchtower would take care of them and provide a home nearby Bethel for them to live in. I had to think quickly and reported that my father would never go for that as he did not like New York City.

Before leaving, I spent time on one more research project. Harry authorized me to create a package of information, alerting and proving to the Governing Body that we had a serious sexual child abuse problem within the organization. Two weeks after I left headquarters in January 1993, a huge packet of information that I had compiled was delivered by Harry Peloyan to each one of the Governing Body members.

When I returned back to my home in Tennessee, I continued to do research for the Writing Department. On my own initiative, I studied the breadth and scope of the sexual child abuse problem in other religions and among society at large. I thought I could be of some use to those at Watchtower who desired a change in child abuse policies.

I was greatly relieved when another letter was received by all Bodies of Elders in the U.S., dated, February 3, 1993. It appeared that my work had reaped results, as the letter actually discussed information I included in the package for Governing Body members. In the letter, elders were instructed on how to help individuals with memories of abuse. And, seeking professional help and reporting of abuse to the authorities was not to be spoken of disparagingly by the elders.

However, much to my horror, after being home a few months, I learned that within the congregations in our area there were several molestation accusations. It was disturbing to know that these cases were dealt with secretly by untrained elders.

New Clumsy Policies

Within a few months after I returned home from Bethel, I asked several elders and congregation members who I personally knew the following question: "How many publicized child abuse cases, along with details, do you remember happening in the local JW community during the last 10 years?" The total number was 14. This did not include the confidential cases reported to the elders and buried in congregation files because there wasn't a second witness to the accuser's molestation.

I shared that information with a Watchtower staff writer and he thought it might be helpful if I wrote a letter to J. R. Brown, the Watchtower's media spokesman, to express my appreciation for the October 8, 1993 Awake! article, "Protect Your Children." When I wrote that letter in December, I requested more articles like it and included information about the "14 cases", thinking Brown would share this news with Watchtower's leadership group.

I also sent a 4-page letter to Lloyd Barry, sharing my findings and begging him to take a second look at Watchtower's policies; to change what needed to be changed to better protect the children. I told him about my concern that too often the predators, who expressed repentance over their acts, were eventually put back into their position of authority in the congregation. Consequently, they were also in a position to molest more children, which many of them did.

But my advice fell on deaf ears, because I learned from friends in the Writing Department that 6 of the 12 GB members—Ted Jaracz, Karl Klein, Albert Shroeder, George Gangas, Milton Henschel and Carey Barber—had backed away from taking supportive and compassionate positions toward abuse victims. And, nothing was being done to remove known molesters from ministerial positions.

When the rights of an organization trump basic human rights, only bad things can happen as Jon Atack explains on pages 59-60, #9.

Nothing was done about this situation until January 1997, when a Watchtower article, "Abhor What Is Wicked," reported that *the organization* would not allow anybody who had a history of molestation to hold a position of responsibility in a *congregation*. But it added: "If he [molester] seems to be repentant, he will be encouraged to make *spiritual progress*, share in the *field service* ..." This was exactly the opposite of my request to restrict their religious *field service activity*.

In addition, there was a loophole in the policy statement. "... no known molester could hold a position of authority in the organization". The key word, "known" was the way molesters stayed in positions of authority. If they weren't "known" as molesters to the congregation or to the community, they were not removed. This information is found in the March 14, 1997 letter "To All Bodies of Elders." In that same letter, it stated "Others may have been guilty of child molestation before they were baptized. The *bodies of elders* should not query these individuals."

I knew who too many of these "individuals" were, which made the statement even more horrific. They were men convicted of child sexual molestation, incarcerated in prisons across the US, and converted after studying the Bible with JW elders, who were active in the JW "prison ministry." These were the men "known" in the "community" mentioned in the letter. After release from prison and baptism, many of them went on to molest the children of the divorced JW women they married.

If that wasn't enough, I had a huge problem with *the two-witness to child abuse rule*, because that was the reason elders gave victims as to why they would not believe the accusation or report the abuse to the police.

When I first became aware of sexual child abuse in the Watchtower organization, I didn't comprehend the scope or harm of the "two-witness" Bible teaching, as it was applied to accusations of molestation. It was only after 1997, when I discovered that the requirement of two witnesses to a molestation protected molesters.

Suppose the accused person denied the charge and the accuser was the only witness to the crime? The elders were instructed to explain to the accuser that nothing more could be done. Hence, the one accused was to be viewed as an innocent person, and not to be spoken against to those not involved in the matter, or the accuser could be opened to a counter charge of slander.

Further, the victim was to be pacified with assurances that the matter could be safely left in Jehovah's hands and if the perpetrator was guilty, eventually his sins would catch up with him. It was actually the misuse of scripture by JWs which kept molesters hidden and put children at risk. - *WATCHTOWER* - November 1, 1995, pgs. 28-29 and August 15, 1997, pg. 28.

The World Outside

Returning home to Tennessee at the beginning of 1993, I continued to do research for the Writing Department, as an official outside researcher until the middle of 1996. In 1994, I wrote a multi-media educational software program for children ages 3 – 8. It was called *Bug Adventure* and received national attention in magazines such as Newsweek. I also did some research and wrote an article for the local Historical Society.

Bug Adventure

This program is crawling with bugs.

Take an interactive journey into the creepy, crawly, flitting, flying, fantastic world of bugs. Watch close-up, candid movies of bugs doing their amazing bug things. Play guessing games with "gee whiz" facts and eyeball benders. Or grab your special glasses to examine bugs in the awesome 3-D lab.
PC CD-ROM $69.95
PC 3.5" disk $49.95

To keep myself busy from thinking about the past, I took a part-time job. However, since the cover-up of child sexual abuse continued, I could not in good conscience support any of the JW activities or meetings. So the members saw less and less of me until I left the JW group early 1998.

It was then that I did something I'd wanted to do for years. Putting my anxiety aside, I took a number of tests at a local community college. After that, I received a scholarship, which gave me the strength to go ahead with my life without my JW friends from all over the world. I knew they would shun me when they realized I was no longer one of them. But, going to college was how I discovered there was life outside of Watchtower and I learned to value myself as a person.

At that time, my husband and I had been married for 39 years. We never kept secrets from one another. Trust and respect were the backbone to our successful marriage. Therefore, Joe accepted my exit from what I now know is a pseudo-religion. He was fully aware that I couldn't accept Watchtower's child sexual abuse policies and believed JW leaders were encouraging elders to: 1) *not* report the crime of child sexual abuse; and 2) telling parents/victims to *not* report these crimes directly to the authorities.

My immediate JW family did not abandon me, at least not then. In the beginning, they were okay with me leaving the organization. In fact, two of them left with me. Those who stayed JWs, including Joe, just stopped talking with me about religion. My son and daughter-in-law talked with me because I was not disfellowshipped. My husband was still an elder and the other elders did not have any idea why I left the religion and were reluctant to ask him. I also didn't say anything negative to anyone about the Watchtower organization, so I was not perceived as a threat.

For over a year after I officially left the organization, I still believed that I would die at Armageddon. As strange as that may sound, Watchtower's psychological manipulation was still at play in my mind. I remember telling a JW, who wanted to help me come back, that I knew I wouldn't survive Armageddon (an induced phobia), but I'd prefer that over ignoring a serious injustice to even one JW child, who could be victimized in the future if I came back and did nothing.

I would later learn how the mind can be manipulated to believe things like "Armageddon" long after a person leaves a high-control cult-like group, as Jon Atack explains on pages 60-61, #10.

Bill Bowen

Toward the end of 2000, a friend of mine saw on a JW-related internet discussion group, a post written by an elder asking if any other elders had a problem like he had just encountered. He had just discovered the congregation's presiding overseer had admitted to molestation some years previously. Since the congregation had no knowledge of the crime, the man remained in his position.

My friend corresponded with this elder and so did I. I told this man about the huge international problem of molestation among JWs and how it was addressed within the organization, and it was a shocking revelation to him. Soon the elder, Bill Bowen, resigned his position in January 1, 2001 and went public over this issue.

The media coverage, in Bill's home state of Kentucky about his resignation as an elder over the child abuse issue, was very impressive. This led to considerable brainstorming about creating an internet website to bring more attention to the problem. Soon, Bill adopted the name his wife suggested, http://silentlambs.org/.

The new website was designed so that victims of child sexual molestation by JW perpetrators could report their stories online. Within weeks there were 1,000 stories. After four years, there were close to 6,000 stories.

Publicity and Excommunication

Although I had not yet revealed myself publicly, within weeks, Bill and I were on a plane to New York City, about to be interviewed by NBC's *Dateline*. *Dateline* was keen to report Watchtower's child sexual abuse problems, but wanted to validate our claims. After doing this, *Dateline* scheduled several taping interviews and offered Watchtower equal time to refute our accusations, which Watchtower denied.

After several delays, the program was set for airing on television for May 28, 2002, and Watchtower was informed of this. Watchtower then quickly notified the local elders to schedule *judicial hearings* for Bill and myself. At my hearing in early May, I was charged with causing divisions within the organization, as they wanted to censor me. But I disproved the charge, as I had not yet caused any divisions.

Within days the local elders scheduled a second judicial hearing with concocted charges. I declined to attend that meeting because it was futile—if I disproved the charges, they would just come up with new ones. So I was disfellowshipped on May 19, 2002. I asked for an appeal hearing, but declined to attend when I was informed that the judicial hearing would have to be held in a nearby motel room with 6 elders and me, and my attorney would *not* be allowed to attend.

Bill Bowen and I were disfellowshipped shortly before *Dateline* was broadcast. In this way, JW viewers would not believe our story. One of Watchtower's doctrines is that disfellowshipped and former members are to be viewed as unrepentant sinners—apostates—thereby muting and censoring us to believing JWs.

When you are being manipulated and locked into a cult-like mind set, it is easy for loyal JWs to follow orders without questioning, as Bonnie Zieman explains on pages 61-62, #11.

Watchtower sent a letter to all U.S. congregations the week before *Dateline* was aired. My husband was at the meeting when it was read. While my name and concerns about Watchtower's child abuse policies were never mentioned, the letter informed members that no organization better protects children than Watchtower. That fake news was the straw that broke the camel's back, as Joe knew it was not true. So after the meeting, he handed the presiding elder his keys to the *Kingdom Hall* and told him that he was resigning.

Joe was asked to submit a letter of resignation, which he did. He gave a copy to each elder and sent a copy to two Governing Body members. He subsequently was disfellowshipped July 2002, because he defended me in his resignation letter. He also stated his views about the child abuse situation, which were not the same as the Watchtower's. Like me, Joe's major complaint was that child sexual abuse was a crime and should be reported to the authorities and not to the elders.

In trying to defend itself, Watchtower publicly libeled me to reporters, saying that the judicial hearing was called because I was a sinner; not because I was going to be on *Dateline*. They blatantly lied, saying they didn't know I was going to appear on the program. When asked by reporters what scripture Watchtower used to disfellowship me, a Watchtower spokesperson said it was 1 Corinthians 5:11, 12. Here Paul commands the congregation to remove the wicked man who is greedy, a fornicator, an idolater, a reviler, a drunkard, or an extortioner.

I did not commit any of those sins, so I filed a defamation lawsuit in November 2002. Unfortunately, the court ruled that my complaint was barred by the ecclesiastical abstention doctrine in the State of Tennessee. A big mistake had been made by my attorney on how he framed the complaint. While I was disappointed in the ruling, I decided to dedicate the rest of my life to try to change the Watchtower policy that violates basic human rights, especially for children

My Break with Bill Bowen

I will always be grateful for Bill Bowen's chutzpah and tenacity. *Dateline's* coverage of Watchtower's child abuse problems would not have seen the light of day without him. But after working with him for two years, it was time to go our separate ways. I have always been a stickler for good research and getting the facts right 100% of the time. However, I wish Bill well, but I cannot support his current work or silentlambs.org as a viable way to bring about change in Watchtower's child sexual abuse policies.

An Unstoppable Advocate for Child Protection

One of the most heartbreaking consequences of my advocacy for child protection was that our son, Lance, decided to shun Joe and me. He told the press I did a "noble" thing trying to protect JW children. However, he did not believe I did the right thing by going public. Apparently, I broke the 11th commandment, the most important one for Jehovah's Witnesses: "Thou shalt not commit publicity".

Bonnie Zieman explains on pages 62-63, #12, how and why people like Lance can shun their own mother and father when they are members of a high-control group like Watchtower.

Lance was told that I misunderstood Watchtower's policies, "and, by my actions," caused thousands of people to leave the organization. Hence, these walk-away JWs were going to die at Armageddon. I was responsible for their deaths.

It has been over 15 years since we have seen our son, daughter-in-law and their child, our grandchild. If we send any mail to them, it is always returned unopened. In addition, we know Lance and his wife, Wendy, have a second child, a girl, who remains faceless and nameless to Joe and me.

When I look back over my life from when I was baptized as one of JWs at age 14, it amazes me where that first step led to. My desire as a woman in the Watchtower organization was to help people understand the spiritual mysteries of life, in line of course with Watchtower's interpretation. But after leaving, my goal is: To help people understand the mystery, at least to me, of why Watchtower just does not change a very bad policy to protect its members, particularly children.

The Last 15 years of my Life as an *Uncensored* Activist

While my head tells me that I am an historian, my heart tells me that I am activist. For the last 15 years of my life I have spent at least 2,000 hours a year, without recompense, to educate the public about a Watchtower policy that does not protect children from pedophiles. I have also been able to help victims of child sexual abuse find legal recourse and psychological support.

My biggest accomplishment was putting together a CD, Secrets of Pedophilia in an American Religion. On the CD, there are 5,000 pages of information, which expose Watchtower policies that don't protect children; and, policies that favor protection of Watchtower's organization over the rights of children. This information can be accessed at my website, http://watchtower-documents.org/, and is free of charge.

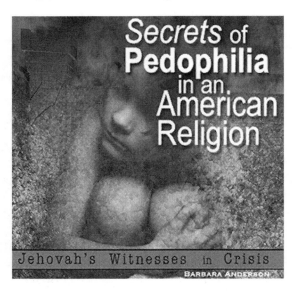

In 2007, shortly after the CD was released to the public, I was asked to appear on the NBC Nightly News with Brian Williams. I flew to Washington DC, where I was interviewed for a three-minute segment that was aired around the world. If you are interested, that interview can be accessed on my website at http://watchtowerdocuments.org/evidence-supports-jehovahs-witness-allegations-msnbc/.

I have spent countless hours talking with journalists from around the world. I have been featured in several well-produced documentary films and have spent hundreds of hours being interviewed by television reporters in the USA, Canada and Europe. As well, I have assisted many lawyers, like Jeff Anderson, Irwin Zalkin, Greg Love and Kimberly Norris (Love & Norris) to adjudicate justice for the victims of child molestation.

In 2009, I visited 5 countries talking to officials at the Vatican in Italy; speaking on the Vatican radio; meeting with governmental officials in Paris; speaking at an ICSA Conference at the University of Geneva in Switzerland, specifically addressing the subject of institutional child sexual abuse in the JW organization.

I am especially proud of the seed I helped plant in 2009 with Steven Unthank. It germinated with the 2017 Australian Commissions report, citing Watchtower's negligence to protect children in Australia over the last 50 years.

Today, I'm honored to work with people like Roger and Karin Bentley and Robert Atkinson, who are helping change laws in California to protect children from abuse.

None of this would be possible without the passion and help from modern-day heroes like Kimberly Norris, Alan Feuerbacher, Randy Watters, Jim Penton, Peter Gregerson, Ray Franz, Joy Grant, Roberto di Stefano, John Hoyle; and of course, my personal hero and husband, Joe Anderson.

I also want to thank the hundreds of people who have come forward asking me how they can help the cause. These are people who don't want their names to be shared with the public. Many of them are and were Jehovah's Witnesses concerned about the lack of protection for the children in their congregations.

While it's a baby step in the right direction, in 2016 Watchtower stopped requiring victims of child molestation to make their allegations in the presence of the alleged abusers, during the investigation and judicial committee process. While this may sound like peanuts, people unfamiliar with the cult-like practices of JWs, it was a BIGGIE to get Watchtower to stop this barbaric practice. But it is still only a small step in what Watchtower must yet do to protect JW children in their congregations around the world.

My Work Continues

While Richard and I were putting together the finishing touches for this book, I received a call from David Gambacorta, a reporter for the Philadelphia Enquirer. He was writing an important story on JWs and child abuse and we talked for 2 1/2 hours. His story will be published on April 26, 2018 at http://www.philly.com.

During the same week, a reporter from a highly acclaimed weekly magazine called me. She was preparing a list of preliminary questions and wanted my advice. She was working on questions she would show her boss in order to get permission to write a major story on Watchtower's policy on reporting of child molestation.

Before that reporter called, I received a Polish YouTube video link from an ex-JW, who told me that information on my website caused both him and his wife to leave the organization two years previously. Now they are activists, trying to change laws about child sexual abuse in Poland. On my email reply, I suggested that he and other activists talk with the Polish Congress about the Statute of Limitations in that country.

I have also been busy for the last few months working with film-makers on two hard-hitting documentaries, although I don't know yet when they will air.

A Call to Action

While I have helped bring about change in how Watchtower treats cases of child sexual abuse, that is not enough. I would like to see more results.

I call on the Watchtower organization (JW.ORG) and governmental legislators around the world to help do the following:

1. Abolish the rule which requires two eyewitnesses to accusations of child sexual abuse before a child is believed
2. Report accusations of child sexual abuse to the authorities
3. Abolish the Statute of Limitations law for child sexual abuse
4. Abolish non-disclosure laws related to child sexual abuse
5. Reform mandatory reporting laws for child sexual abuse
6. Make background checks mandatory for people working with children
7. Stop treating it as consensual sex, when a 'willing' JW minor, age 14-16, is sexually involved with someone a few years older (Under law, a minor cannot be 'willing'. Any sexual act with a minor is rape, because the minor has no right to consent.)
8. Instruct JW elders that child sexual abuse will haunt victims for the rest of their lives, and often leads to devastating consequences.

As stated above, it is imperative to inform authorities that most JW elders view it as consensual sex, when a so-called 'willing JW minor', age 14-16, is sexually involved with someone who is a few years older. Hence, there is little effort to report this behavior to the police. Even if they both consented, it should not be treated as a sin. It is a crime!

We need to educate JW.ORG, its rank and file, and the public-at-large that not only do victims of child sexual abuse experience long-standing psychological damage from maltreatment; it is particularly devastating when a sexually transmitted disease occurs. If caregivers of victims of sexual abuse are not encouraged to go to the authorities, because the perpetrator is a JW and reporting would bring reproach on the religion, the child's physical health could be seriously compromised.

It is also important to increase the awareness of politicians and the media about the need for legislative ideas to reform statutes that prevent perpetrators from abusing more than one victim. One such grass-root movement that is producing results is Stop Child Abuse: Advocates for Reform and Safety (SCAARS.CA on Facebook).

Another grass-root movement, which has been extremely effective in creating awareness of Watchtower's long history of treating child sexual abuse as a sin and not a crime, is Reclaimed Voices. They are located in the Netherlands and have been able to attract the services of an effective Dutch attorney, Nico Meijering.

You can help me organize a new, more comprehensive group initiative, which will be focused on all forms of child abuse. Please see the Call to Action from Roger Bentley, and related prospectus, on pages 81 – 85. If you are interested in helping build a worthy cause, please contact me at Ima.Friend@gmail.com.

The general public needs to be aware of the high number of suicides among born-in JWs, particularly during their teenage years and young adulthood. Children growing up in this highly-controlled better-than-everyone-else culture have a difficult time going it alone in a world they have been taught to fear and despise.

Please help me end the inhumane practice of shunning, which when applied to victims of sexual abuse, cuts the victim off from the essential support of friends and family. This is an outrageous form of secondary abuse for the victim. To learn more about the debilitating effects of shunning after being sexually abused or leaving a high-control group, visit: https://bonniezieman.com/mandated-shunning/.

I will continue to be an outspoken critic of Watchtower policies that protect sexual predators and unduly influence JWs to believe their policies are Bible-based and inspired from God. I will also partner with the Open Minds Foundation, as its goal is to educate the public about the adverse effects of undue influence.

The overall mission for Open Minds is to safeguard society, particularly young people, against psychological manipulation by predatory groups and predators. This manipulation is manifest in the form of propaganda, fake news, unrealistic promises and telling parents not to report child molestation to the authorities.

I, along with Open Minds, support free thought and independent, albeit informed, choice. Everyone should be allowed the opportunity to unlock their potential to manage their own affairs and to realize their competence.

You can join me by supporting the Open Minds Foundation and making tax-free financial contributions to this charitable group. Your gifts will also help provide the resources for many of the worthwhile projects that I'm committed to. Please visit their website at: https://www.openmindsfoundation.org/.

Commentary from Bonnie Zieman, M.Ed. & Jon Atack

Bonnie and Jon will comment here on how/why Watchtower unduly influences its members so that they are willing to abdicate their critical thinking skills and to even violate the basic human rights of non-believers as follows:

1. From page 24, Bonnie comments on how 13-year-old Barbara was being manipulated

(How could I at 13 years of age make such a significant decision like that? What was I thinking?)

It is troubling to read of a 13-year-old child being persuaded to make such a pivotal choice at that stage of her life. While life circumstances may make children vulnerable to the lure of what they think is a caring community, coupled with high ideals, and the promise of living forever on a paradise earth, the prefrontal cortex of a child is not developed enough to weigh the long-term implications of such a decision.

The prefrontal cortex area is the executive function of the brain, which controls one's ability to differentiate between competing opinions (good/better/best), prioritize, predict outcomes, and make complex decisions and long-term plans.

At the age of 13, Barbara, like any child of that age, had not fully developed the use of the "executive functions" of her brain, which would have enabled her to filter, assess, and select a life path. Most neurologists agree that the prefrontal cortex is not fully developed until about 25 years of age.

It is understandable that an unhappy child could be seduced with promises of truth, friendship, community, and everlasting life in paradise. What child would not want to step right into a fairy tale? However, Barbara, as any 13-year-old, would need several years of further brain development and maturation before she could, or should, make a decision that would have such serious consequences for the rest of her life.

Little did she know, as she is now able to articulate, that she was joining an "aggressive, controversial religion"—a cult—with many unconventional beliefs, illusions, promises, and practices that would eventually threaten and steal much of what she held dear.

2. From page 25, Jon comments on how the mind can rationalize a false prophecy

Although the 1975 date set by JWs for the Apocalypse (Armageddon) came and went, Joe and I were not deterred. And for me, I had personally invested 21 years of my life in the religion and I was not about to throw in the towel.

In the early 1950s, psychologist Leon Festinger infiltrated students into a group called the Seekers. Their leader, Marian Keech, led her followers to believe that she was channeling a disembodied spirit called Sananda, who told her that the human race was about to be destroyed in a great flood that would split the American continent in two. Only those who were faithful to her would be saved, by a spaceship from Sananda's home planet.

Festinger predicted that believers who travelled for the rendezvous with the spaceship would become more, rather than less, fervent. They would believe that their faith had averted the catastrophe. In his book, *When Prophecy Fails*, Festinger explained the now well-proven theory of cognitive dissonance. **When our convictions are challenged, we usually refuse the conflicting evidence** and give even more weight to those convictions.

There is an inertia to belief: we tend to keep moving in the direction we have chosen. **We believe in our certainties, even though they are usually based more upon feelings, as opposed to reason.** Barbara felt that Watchtower had the Truth, and that overwhelmed her reasoning.

3. From page 28, Jon comments on control of information

The transcript of Maria Russell's cross-examination was not given to me to read and I did not question why I was not allowed to read it. But years later, I did read it and was amazed at how Maria's problems with Russell were misrepresented to JWs in Watchtower literature.

High-control groups are very careful to restrict information. They will ridicule or dismiss anything that does not agree with their dogma. Once we have accepted a source of information as authoritative, it can be very difficult to accept any contradiction of that source. We do not live in a society that encourages critical thinking; there is an emphasis upon obedience rather than intelligent questioning. So, Barbara accepted the Watchtower Society's decision without realizing that she had a right to all the information. This is not simply a matter of cultic influence; very few people are able to resist the groupthink of the society to which they belong.

In a high-control group, the decisions of the leadership are paramount; information is controlled to the benefit of the group and the detriment of the member, and any doubt is considered impure. This is the aspect of thought reform called the *demand for purity* by Robert Jay Lifton. It becomes psychologically difficult to question anything in the judgmental atmosphere of a cult, where doubt is seen as sinful or demonic. The doctrine of the group is accepted even over actual experiences, which Lifton called *doctrine over person* or *ideology over experience*.

Human history is littered with instances where groups of

otherwise rational people have accepted unproven and irrational dogma. The Behaviorist doctrine dominated psychology in the US for decades, until its central tenet–that nothing could be known about the human mind–was defeated by researchers into neurophysiology and cognitive science. This happened as recently as the 1970s. Groupthink can overwhelm even the brightest minds.

4. From page 29, Bonnie explains how cults get a person to stop thinking

(I was not ready to believe negative information about Watchtower, as I had been programmed to reject it as a people problem and not Watchtower's problem.)

Barbara held a position within the headquarters of Jehovah's Witnesses that gave her access to much more information than the average JW – particularly any JW female. As Barbara conducted assigned research for the Watchtower, she also made discoveries about "objectionable behaviors" on the part of some of those in positions of authority in the organization–discoveries about people, attitudes, and activities inside the group that were discordant with what she believed to be true.

Barbara then experienced what researcher Leon Festinger named "cognitive dissonance"–new information contradicting all she had been led to believe. When anyone experiences disharmony in beliefs or cognitions, there is a strong inner compulsion to find a way to explain, harmonize or rationalize the competing sets of information or, if necessary, simply dismiss the new discordant belief. Until humans find a way to make the relationship between the two discordant sets of information harmonious, they will feel distinctly anxious. That anxiety will push them to explain away, rationalize or reject any information that threatens or disagrees with what they already believe.

Barbara's psyche found its way to dismiss the discordant information about the behaviors observed within the Watchtower in order to minimize both conscious and unconscious anxiety. She eliminated the palpable discomfort of cognitive dissonance by formulating a rationale for the unpalatable discoveries, naming the aberrant behaviors as being due to human failings ("people junk") rather than organizational failings or errors of dogma. By so doing, Barbara was able to minimize the anxiety caused by cognitive dissonance and maintain her allegiance to the organization...for a while.

5. From page 30, Jon explains how cults justify why they are above the law

High-control groups and their members believe that they are above the law. Religious cults believe that they must obey what they consider to be the laws of God. This makes sense, if you believe in God. However, much of the time, the law is not biblical, but an invention of the cult. This is definitely the case with Watchtower, which has created a Kafkaesque system that denies proper justice to its followers by the use of under-educated tribunal members.

All too often, there is a justification that allowing scrutiny by the real legal system will lead to disrepute for the group, so we have seen cover-ups of abuse in many groups. The truth is that any organization that conceals criminal activity has in effect become a criminal organization. Members are put into conflict with their own morality by demanding loyalty to the organization as if it were loyalty to God. Loyalty to conscience is vital to good mental health.

6. From page 31, Jon explains why psychologists are "no-no" in cults

Cults cannot afford to allow members access to psychotherapy, because it will inevitably lead them to question their fixed dogma. Scientologists are told that all psychotherapists are part of a conspiracy to rule the universe. Krishnas are told that anyone who questions their doctrine is a "deadly demon". The creation of an out-group, considered deviant, is vital to the defense of monstrous ideas. The Nazis called their opponents: *untermensch*– "underlings"–who were racially and socially inferior. In a truly democratic society, we must have access to all opinions and be allowed to consider them for ourselves, rather than accepting propaganda and spin.

7. From page 32, Bonnie explains how cognitive dissonance was working in Barbara's mind

(This was new and scary for me. I could not figure it out, although my primal brain was telling me to take flight.)

By this time in her story, Barbara had come across information about troubling systemic patterns in the JW organization–the cover-up of pervasive child sexual abuse in congregations across the United States. Her sense of solid grounding in the beliefs of the religion were shaken by such discoveries.

Barbara now had proof that the organization was not dealing properly with reported cases of child sexual abuse, and that the JW perpetrators of this abuse were not being reported to the authorities. If that was not enough, the congregations and the parents in them were not being warned about child predators operating in their midst.

This was information that a person could not dismiss or rationalize, as one would with 'everyday' cognitive dissonance. Allegiance to a religion could not hold up when paired up against concerns for the safety of minors in the group, all across the country.

As Barbara considered taking on the role of a whistle blower, fears for her own psychological safety within the organization arose. Her body was even alerting her with "sick feelings" that she could be subjected to an unwarranted judicial hearing, public condemnation and expulsion from the organization. She knew that the worst result would be the loss of her family and friends.

Anyone in this kind of situation would surely find themselves in a state of inner turmoil. On the one hand their autonomic nervous system would be telling them and preparing them to "fight" by standing up and exposing the wrongs in the organization, while on the other hand it would be pushing them to "flee" to get away from the situation that was becoming such a threat, or to "freeze" (withdraw, collapse, or shut down) in order to preserve their way of life and precious relationships.

This must have been a horrendous crisis of conscience: would Barbara choose loyalty to the religion for which she had sacrificed so much, or the safety of young children? It was a crisis that could only end up puncturing the ever-present undue influence to rationalize or dismiss information that contradicted or exposed the Watchtower.

If Barbara rationalized participating in the cover-up to protect the reputation of the organization (which is always accentuated as a prime value in the group), how could she live with the knowledge of rampant child sexual abuse left unaddressed? On a personal level, how could she risk losing all she held dear?

8. From page 33, Jon explains about the lack of accountability

When they cannot make sense of a decision, members of high-control groups rely either on the more developed understanding of those above them in the hierarchy or upon their own intuition. Intuition should always be checked against the facts. Superiors are above criticism in a high-control group. One clear sign of a destructive group is the lack of accountability.

It is a dreadful mistake to believe without evidence, but we all defer to authority sometimes; members of high-control groups defer more often, and at times completely. Predatory people are very good at putting on a good show–criminal psychopaths often fool parole boards and can convince even highly trained psychologists that they will not re-offend. We need to take responsibility for all of our actions and beliefs; it is dangerous to abandon our own moral autonomy.

9. From page 36, Jon explains the rights of an organization vs basic human rights

I also expressed my concern that within the congregations, too often predators, who expressed repentance over their acts, were eventually put back into their position of authority. Consequently, they were in a position to molest more children, which many of them did. But my advice fell on deaf ears.

Forgiveness is fundamental to a decent society, but it can be a bad mistake to forgive and forget; we need to forgive and *remember*. Predators will go through the motions of repentance, but repeat their offense just as soon as backs are turned.

The Watchtower Society is mired in its own groupthink: they believe that once a sin has been confessed it will not be repeated. The truth is that child molesters should never again be trusted with the care of children.

10. From page 41, Jon explains why fears of Armageddon can linger

Prophecies of catastrophe are as old as religion itself. Followers are presented with a simple choice: follow the dogma, or die in the coming apocalypse. Beliefs of this kind led to the Crusades and the Millennarian movements of the medieval period. In *The Pursuit of the Millennium*, historian Norman Cohn relates the many massacres of those times, brought about by hysterical belief in the End Times.

Once we accept an apocalyptic doctrine, we have no choice but to follow it. The Aztecs believed that without freshly plucked human hearts, the sun would no longer rise. They weren't about to take that risk.

Destructive cults fill their members with the same degree of fear. They induce phobias, especially about leaving the group. Moonies are told that all of their ancestors will go to hell if they leave the group. Scientologists are told that they will "lose their immortality".

Watchtower fills its members with dread that they will die at Armageddon, if they fail to follow its rules. This fear of an abrupt, violent death often persists for years after a believer has left. It is a source of post-traumatic stress. Sufferers will wake in panic with nightmares. The very mention of Armageddon can cause their palms to sweat and the heart to palpitate. These are normal stress reactions,which we all suffer to some extent, but with ex-members, they can be overwhelming.

11. From page 42, Bonnie explains why people blindly follow instructions from cult leaders

(When you are being manipulated and locked into a cult-like mind set, it is easy for loyal JWs to follow orders without questioning, as Bonnie Zieman explains.)

Barbara did courageously blow the whistle on Watchtower abuse, neglect of duty of care, and the cover-up of child sexual abuse occurring in congregations across the United States. She did so knowing that the consequences for herself and her family would be shattering. She was not wrong on either count.

The "kangaroo court" was held. Barbara's pleas to protect children in congregations across the country were dismissed by the Watchtower. They then made an effort to invalidate Barbara's revelations about pervasive child sexual abuse by labelling her a liar and an apostate, expelling her from the organization, and pressuring anyone still a member of the religion to ignore and ostracize her.

The thought control exercised in this organization is powerful. Orders to not listen to or to dismiss anything said by someone who leaves the group are followed without question. It is often suggested in their study materials that such people have succumbed to the influence of Satan and everything they say is part of Satan's plan to destroy God's one true organization.

Millions of Jehovah's Witnesses were "strongly advised" that to watch the Dateline program featuring Barbara and Bill would not be something devoted, spiritually-minded servants of the true God would want to do. They were asked questions like, *"Did they really want to expose themselves to Satanic influence and lies by listening to apostates lie on television?"*–and millions, in lemming-like loyalty, refused to watch the Dateline program that could expose the lies and failings of Watchtower.

The Watchtower's thought control over their members is so strong, that they do not even have to issue explicit orders saying, "*Do not watch Dateline on this date.*" They simply ask seemingly innocent questions about whether doing such a thing is what a loyal servant of Jehovah would do. They know the answer in each member's mind will be "*Of course not.*" The mind-control is so powerful they only have to hint at or suggest what they want their members to do. This use of mere suggestions allows them to publicly deny that they give orders to members about what they can or cannot watch or read.

Barbara was well aware of how the Watchtower would portray her and how she would be treated as a result. Yet she courageously stood up against child sexual abuse within the group and spoke truth to power.

12. From page 44, Bonnie explains why Jehovah's Witnesses are willing to shun their family

(Surely Lance would not shun his own mother and father? Bonnie Zieman explains how and why this happens in a high-control culture like Jehovah's Witnesses.)

It is quite incomprehensible to understand how a family member can reject another because they change beliefs or speak out about injustice. Yet, millions of loving families have been torn asunder by the Watchtower's policy to disfellowship and shun anyone who does not conform to their beliefs and practices.

The only possible explanation is that members of this organization have been so indoctrinated that they must obey all Watchtower rules and guidelines that they mindlessly conform even at the cost of precious family ties. Part of this indoctrination includes a persistent dehumanization of anyone who is not one of Jehovah's Witnesses.

Once the member has been influenced to put anyone who is not a "true believer" in another category of human, (a category that says they will soon be destroyed by Jehovah anyway) it becomes easier to abuse them with acts of rejection, exclusion and shunning.

Shunning a parent or child is the prime example of the pervasive indoctrination, dehumanization, mind-control, or cult-programming in this organization which influences good people to act against their own best interests and to make decisions that negatively affect their family and future.

Barbara's son seemed able to exercise his own judgment about his mother's actions when he named her wanting to protect children as "noble" to the press. Unfortunately, he could not stand up against Watchtower's requirement to exclude and shun her—especially since she was publicly exposing Watchtower's underbelly.

Barbara's son seemed to be so under Watchtower's spell that he was/is willing to obey their rules that result in the loss of a loving relationship with his mother, and as life moved on, to even deny his own children a relationship with their grandmother. What a monumental sacrifice for any organization to expect of their members.

Ostracism is an unjust and inhumane requirement of the Watchtower Society that negatively impacts both those who are shunned and those who shun. This inhumane requirement could only be a part of the governance of a leadership exhibiting anti-social patterns which include a profound absence of conscience, remorse, or shame.

Impact of Sexual Abuse on Children in JW.ORG

Child sexual abuse has severe short-term and long-term consequences for the victim. When a child being abused realizes that "fight" or "flight" is not an option, their nervous system may help them deal with the horror, pain, and fear of death with a "freeze" response. With a freeze response the child's mind and nervous system shut down, withdraw, or even seemingly leave the body, to escape to a 'safe' place. The latter option is called "dissociation".

Immediately after the abuse the child's terrorized body/mind, again in a normal self-protective response, may suppress or deny that the abuse even happened – their mind being unable to comprehend that such inhumane acts are possible. These hard-wired, protective responses make it difficult for a child to talk about or report the abuse. Even if the child can articulate that the violation happened, they may have no words to describe the horrors and terrors experienced. Their mind may not have absorbed specific details of where, when, how, etc.

If the abuse is ongoing and the child feels under constant threat they are then continually flooded with and disturbed by stress hormones. Without the judgment and perspective of an adult brain, the child may think they are somehow to blame and that they will experience more threats to their wellbeing if they dare to report the adult. Trauma expert, Bessel van der Kolk, M.D. says,

"As a result, shame becomes the dominant emotion and hiding the truth the central preoccupation."[1]

If a Jehovah's Witness child is sexually abused by a fellow member of the congregation, it is a terrifying thing to consider reporting the adult to other adults. If congregation elders hear of allegations of sexual abuse, the child, most likely a teenager, will be called before a "judicial committee" to make their accusations in front of three male elders, as is the requirement in all JW congregations. (Before August 1, 2016, the accused offender could be there to challenge the child accuser. Fortunately that is not allowed today.) This is another form of invasive violation for the child victim. Again their self-protective nervous system responses will kick in to help them cope with this further abuse. The elders in these scenarios are so uninformed and ill-equipped to handle such situations that they probably have no comprehension of the harm they are doing to an already abused and suffering child.

The child knows they cannot "fight" back in this meeting. The child knows they are not allowed to "flee" the room. The only response left in this "hearing" is for them to "freeze" – shut down, withdraw internally, or dissociate. In such a state a child is hardly able to provide or prove details of the abuse. Because the JWs use a Bible verse that says two witnesses to any crime are required to substantiate allegations, the pedophile often escapes any consequences and resumes activities in the congregation. Congregants are not informed there is a pedophile in their midst.

The sexually abused child is virtually abandoned and re-abused when they attempt to seek help in this "Christian congregation". They have been terrorized by sexual abuse and then they are re-abused having to try to present their case in a room of male authority figures. In many cases the child victims are discounted, implicitly shamed, and receive no help or supportive direction. The elders running this "kangaroo court" (that has no authority anywhere but in their JW congregation) have absolutely no training in how to treat a victim of sexual abuse–how to ask questions that do not become a further violation. Bessel van der Kolk goes on to say, *"Numerous studies ... have shown that **social support** is*

---

1   "The Body Keeps The Score: Brain, Mind, and Body in the Healing of Trauma", 2013, Bessel van der Kolk, M.D., page 67 and page 79.

*the most powerful protection against becoming overwhelmed by
stress and trauma...The critical issue is **reciprocity**: being **truly
heard and seen** by the people around us, feeling that we are held
in someone else's mind and heart. For our physiology to calm
down, heal and grow we need a visceral feeling of **safety**."* How
reciprocal and safe are these "judicial meetings" where a sexually
abused child is callously interrogated before their abuser? Support,
healing, and justice for the child are not the primary concern of
this 'tribunal'. Protecting the good name and reputation of their
god, Jehovah inside and outside the congregation is the foremost
concern of the elders.

As well, Watchtower headquarters has made it clear to all elders that the reputation of the organization should be protected at
all costs. For years, allegations of child sexual abuse were rarely,
if ever, reported to police or social services. The pedophile who
did not have two witnesses to his/her abuse freely frequented the
congregation and its activities. The sexually abused child was/
is discredited and, in effect, abandoned. Imagine the emotional
reactions–especially the rage–this discounted, re-victimized child
must now suppress.

Compound childhood abuse such as this can change (if
not damage) structures of the abused child's brain–such as the
amygdala, limbic system, cortex, and hippocampus to name a
few. Research shows that adverse childhood experiences (ACE[2])
impact structures of the brain and neural pathways, and that the
impact continues into adulthood. People abused as a child may
organize their life as if they are still under threat of violation and
trauma, thereby contributing to many long-term physical or mental
health issues, depending on the vulnerabilities of the individual.

There is hope for healing, however, for victims of childhood
sexual abuse in the Jehovah's Witnesses organization. This same
research into adverse childhood experiences reveals that because
of the amazing neuroplasticity of the brain, damage done to it
during childhood sexual abuse can be rewired back to normal
functioning. Talk therapy and other body-based interventions such

2   Research conducted by the American Health Maintenance Organization
Kaiser Permanente and the Centers for Disease Control and Prevention, 1995 –
1997.

as EMDR therapy, trauma release exercises, yoga, breath work, tai chi, mindfulness meditation, drawing, writing, and healthy social engagement, etc. can reboot the nervous system away from a chronic emergency stance and rewire parts of the brain stunted or damaged by the trauma of childhood sexual assault.

Hope for a no tolerance policy of pedophiles and child sexual abuse in the Watchtower organization depends on brave whistle-blowers and activists like Barbara Anderson. We must give her and her initiatives our support, and demand immediate global reform of policies and practices in this international organization, JW.ORG, that have heretofore acted as if they are a law unto themselves.

Bonnie Zieman, 20/01/18

Further Reading:

"Childhood Disrupted: How Your Biography Becomes Your Biology, and How You Can Heal", 2016, Donna Jackson Nakazawa

"Healing Developmental Trauma: How Early Trauma Affects Self-Regulation, Self-Image, and the Capacity for Relationship", 2012, Laurence Heller, Ph.D. and Aline LaPierre, Psy.D.

"Trauma Through a Child's Eyes: Awakening the Ordinary Miracle of Healing, 2006, Peter A. Levine, Ph.D. and Maggie Kline

"Treating Traumatic Stress in Children and Adolescents: How to Foster Resilience through Attachment, Self-Regulation, and Competency", 2010, Margaret E. Blaustein and Kristine M. Kinniburgh

Epilogue

Six years after I left Bethel and one year after I no longer attended meetings, I went back to school. After taking some tests at the local community college, I received a two-year college scholarship. One of the required courses that I had to take was on critical thinking. What I learned in that class was a revelation to me as I did not think I needed to be taught how to think critically.

The book we students had to use was *BEYOND FEELINGS, A Guide to Critical Thinking*, Fifth Edition, by Vincent Ryan Ruggiero. That class was one of the most challenging of all my classes. And I learned to acquire skills to test the accuracy of statements and the soundness of the reasoning that connects them. The major way to do that is to ask questions, something which is frowned upon by Watchtower.

Although I was fading from the Watchtower organization, because of their child abuse policies, I still had not probed deeply into my belief system. I still took what Watchtower had taught me at face value rather than challenging the ideas. Once I applied what I learned in that class to my belief system, I realized the illogicalness of the choice of faith I had made so long ago.

Each of our stories of escape from Watchtower's mental prison is different, but the outcome is the same. We now can exercise our free will; we can ask questions that lead to *discoveries*. For me, out of the Watchtower means life's journey is one big adventure, one that I embarked on when I began to take college classes and felt the exhilaration of discovery.

No wonder Watchtower leaders try to employ persuasive coercion to keep its members from attending university.

Joe and I have not seen our son and his family since we were disfellowshipped in 2002. Our grandson was three then and he will be 19 in September, 2018. We saw a photo of him two years ago and he's a handsome young man.

We were hopeful that someday our son, Lance, and daughter-in-law, Wendy, would come to their senses. But they have become hardened toward us, especially after I appeared on NBC Nightly News in November 2007. We expect that we will never see them again, and that's not an easy thing to think about or write about.

We certainly understand how Watchtower has unduly influenced Lance to turn Joe and I into monsters—apostates. He was in Bethel for 16 years and had a big circle of friends in and out of Bethel, who were also unduly influenced by Watchtower. To Lance and the large well-known JW family in Northern Indiana and Michigan that he married into, we are an embarrassment to him.

Our son is an only child. By marrying into the Bryant family, he gained a large family. His wife has three sisters and one brother. Wendy's brother was a Bethelite assigned to the Service Department. Two of Wendy's sisters, including Wendy, married Bethelite men and joined their husbands at Bethel.

All of those men are now out of Bethel, and probably still elders. Wendy also has several male cousins who were elders. So our son, Lance, has found a Witness niche which he is happy to be part of.

We think and talk about our son and his family often. Although it was difficult the first few years to know that our son chose the Watchtower over us, we have come to terms with it. It helps to think of the good times that we all had together and we try not to dwell on the negatives.

Like many others in the same situation, it is not only our losses that concern us. But it hurts us to think of how much our son has lost by deciding to stay with Watchtower. Even though, before we left the organization, he thought we were wonderful parents. (See the August 8, 1993 Awake!, page 31.) He does not answer our phone calls, and, in the past, sent back any letters or gifts we sent.

There are no words to express how sorry we are that we brought up our son in this deceptive religion. But of course, we can't go back and undo it. Life, however, must go on and Joe and I have found activities that we enjoy and we have learned to embrace our life, even absent our dear son.

In fact, Joe and I just came back from a long motorcycle ride in our beautiful home state of Tennessee. Actually, we love our life out of the Watchtower. It is great having both the time and freedom to make new friends, read thought-provoking books, think for ourselves, and see new sights.

However, as long as we're alive, Joe and I will continue to expose Watchtower's cover-up of child sexual abusers within their ranks.

But wait, there is one more story I want to share with you. It is about a broken promise that Harry Peloyan made to me. He said that he would never allow articles critical of the Catholic Church, related to child abuse, to appear in the Awake! magazine. Since JWs had similar problems, it would be hypocritical to "throw stones" at a group that was doing exactly the same thing as Watchtower.

If Joe and I had remained at headquarters, the April 8, 1993 Awake! would have been placed in our living quarters approximately four weeks before the publishing date and I would have known then that Harry did not keep his word.

If you would like to read more about this story, along with a copy of the Awake! article, a letter that Harry wrote to me and much more, please visit my website at: http://watchtowerdocuments.org/document-library/.

Afterthoughts by Richard Kelly

I have had several people ask me what Barbara is really like. She appears to many as very driven and deeply committed to her cause, which she is. While she is hard-wired to produce worldclass-type research, she is a compassionate activist by choice, who will let nothing get in her way of trying to protect children from abuse.

Knowing that a good picture can say a thousand words, I asked Detroit artist and ex-JW elder Carl Wilson to use his amazing talents to create portraits of Barbara. You have seen his work on display earlier in this book. One was a caricature and the other an impressionist line drawing.

All in all, I have attached four of his portraits in this book. Barbara and I thought about using one of them for the cover page of this book. However, we opted to use an actual photo of Barbara, considering the nature and purpose of this book. More about Carl's work later.

Having worked many hours with Barbara to help tell her story, I want you to know she is a genuine and happy person. Both Barbara and her husband have a great sense of humor. If I would have clocked laugh-time working with Barbara on this book it would have been significant.

It has been a real joy for me to collaborate with Barbara,

helping to tell her story. In fact, I have been tempted on many occasions to share lengthy anecdotal information about Barbara, showcasing the kind of caring and discerning person that she is. But this book would have been way too long had I done so. If I started telling even one of these delightful, detailed stories about her, where would I stop? However, I will give you an interesting tidbit before sharing more of Carl's artistic interpretations of one of my modern-day heroes, Barbara Anderson.

When Barbara was born, she was gifted with a mop-full of jet black curly hair on the top of her head. When her mother saw Barbara for the first time, she was sure the nurse had given her the wrong baby. So she curtly informed the nurse of her mistake as only a good Polish mother can do. A grieving mother who had just lost her baby overheard the accusation and responded quickly. She would be willing to take the child. Upon hearing this, Barbara's mother quickly apologized. A few weeks later, Barbara lost her black curly hair and mother nature showered her with golden threads of Goldilocks-like hair.

Moving forward seventy-plus years, Barbara has aged well. Today's image of her, as seen by highly-skilled artist Carl Wilson, is very special to me. His line drawings and caricatures will give you a unique perspective of this remarkable woman. What do you think about the following portraits?

BARBARA ANDERSON
UNCENSORED

Glossary of JW *Loaded Language* Words used in the Book

Jehovah's Witnesses use words and phrases in unique ways, which make it difficult for non-members to understand. Their jargon consists of many thought-terminating clichés that are intended to alter the members' thought processes so they conform to the group's way of thinking. For example, JWs call their organization **The Truth**. This makes it difficult to doubt the truthfulness of their leadership. Other unique words/phrases found in this book are:

Watchtower's hierarchy

Governing Body members – a group of men who lead Watchtower's worldwide organization; they are responsible for setting policy and beliefs/dogma

Bethelites – men and women who live and work at Bethel—Watchtower's headquarters

Kingdom Ministry Schools – In-house two-week training schools to help JW elders learn Watchtower policies and procedures

overseers (congregation, circuit, district and branch) – men in charge of different groups and elders

elders and the body of elders – a group of men who manage individual congregations

ministerial servants – men who apprentice elders

judicial committee members – three elders in a congregation who are judge and jury for members who are accused of a Watchtower-

type sin or refuse to believe certain doctrines
pioneers – JWs who spent 100 hours (in Barbara's day) a month proselytizing for new members
special pioneers – JWs who spent 150 hours (in Barbara's day) a month proselytizing for new members
brothers and **sisters** – active JWs
publishers – JWs who spend at least one hour a month proselytizing for new members
full-time (volunteer) ministers – men and women who spend their time pioneering or working at Bethel

Unique beliefs, policies and practices

Armageddon – a worldwide apocalyptic battle between God and the devil to occur in our lifetime
144,000 and the remnant – faithful JWs who will live in heaven and rule with Jesus Christ after they die
disfellowshipping – excommunication of a JW
extreme shunning – if you have been disfellowshipped or disassociate, you are to be shunned, although for legal reasons members will rarely use that word (it's something you do and don't say)
door-to-door ministry – JWs proselytizing for new members
return visits/back calls – when interest is shown by someone, a return visit is made to proselytize
shepherding visits/calls and shepherding the flock – visiting with physically or spiritually sick JWs
blood transfusion policy – JWs believe God does not approve of blood transfusions
the new world – in 1935 JWs were taught that faithful JWs will live forever in a paradise earth

Misrepresentation of words

apostates – like the N-word for racial bigots, its Watchtower's A-word for ex-members/believers
bible studies – JWs call it a bible study, but it's really a study of a Watchtower publication
mature Christians – any JW who follows all Watchtower beliefs

and policies

worldly people – anyone who is not a JW

assignments – when a JW is asked to do something it is framed as an "assignment from Jehovah"

privileges – if a JW is asked to do something from a higher-ranking JW it is framed as a "privilege"

serving – any work done as a JW is considered as "serving Jehovah"

spiritual food – verbal or written information coming from Watchtower and its Governing Body

new truths – changes in Watchtower doctrines and policies

theocratic warfare – telling a lie if the information could be damaging to the Watchtower organization

spiritual maturity – is a true believing JW who follows Watchtower's direction 100% of the time

the new personality – when you act and think like Watchtower wants you to

Physical organizational terms

Kingdom Hall or Hall – a church-like meeting place for JWs

congregations – a group of 30 to 120 JWs assigned to worship together under the direction of elders

meetings – talks and discussion groups, which are generally held at a Kingdom Hall

public talks – a talk (sermon) at the Kingdom Hall or assembly that is designed for the public

Bethel – Watchtower's headquarters where its leaders and worker bees live and work

Bethel home – where a person working for Watchtower permanently lives

Service Department – the most powerful department at Bethel; and responsible for managing congregation activities worldwide (All elders and overseers report to this department.)

Writing Department – a department at Bethel in the USA responsible for all written material

the Organization (or Jehovah's organization) – the Watchtower Bible & Tract Society/JW.ORG

assemblies (circuit, district and international) – these are large conventions where great groups of JWs meet
judicial committees and meetings – where all infractions of JW policies and beliefs are adjudicated
New World Translation of the Bible – Watchtower's version of the Bible
Watchtower magazine – the official journal for JWs
Awake! – a magazine that reports on social issues and world events
reporting time in field service – all JWs report their time and results while in the door-to-door ministry.

Common Phrases

- we don't want to bring reproach upon Jehovah's name (Jehovah's organization)
- we put our trust in Jehovah and His organization
- aligning your thinking with the organization (Watchtower)
- Armageddon is just around the corner (or the end is near)
- do you want to die at Armageddon?
- let's wait on Jehovah to resolve the problem
- JWs are the happiest group of people in the world
- if you're not serving Jehovah, you're serving the devil
- who do you love more, Jehovah or your non-believing spouse /children?
- if JWs don't have the truth, then who does?
- JWs are closer to the truth than any other group
- preach the good news of God's kingdom
- conduct unbecoming of a Christian
- the two-witness to child abuse rule
- breaking Caesar's law
- a wife's head is her husband

A Call to Action from Roger Bentley

Earlier in the book Barbara informed you about a grass roots movement that my wife Karin, Robert Atkinson, and I initiated in the state of California. Our goal is to change laws to protect children from abuse, which is a public safety issue facing the citizens of California. We have increased awareness to politicians and the media about the need for legislative ideas to reform statutes that prevent abusers from abusing more than one victim. We call our group, Stop Child Abuse: Advocates for Reform and Safety (SCAARS.CA on Facebook).

But that is not enough. Our challenge now is to expand from a successful regional and narrowly focused SCAARS.CA (we don't want to lose that) to an international and broader focus (all forms of child abuse) SCAARS.ORG. We are interested in exploring ideas on creating a larger organization that could help incubate more grassroots successes like SCAARS.CA and Reclaimed Voices in the Netherlands.

My name is Roger Bentley and I was an active member of a high-control religious institution from 1971 to 2014. The group can be referred to as "Totalistic." I was a true believer until I came into conflict with policy and doctrinal changes. When I exercised my basic human rights to disagree with "official organizational" teachings and legal tactics, I was labeled an apostate. As a result, all family and friends loyal to this organization are required not to speak to me. They cannot even say a greeting to me, which has prompted me to speak out about the hidden dangers that this group conceals from their members and the public.

Our SCAARS group/movement seeks to combine recovery from leaving a "high control group" (cult), with advocacy for improved laws to deal with child sex abuse, and other important areas, like shunning, blood transfusions, and sexual harassment. Human rights as well as First Amendment issues will naturally be taken into consideration.

Currently being discussed with the California Senate staff are the issues of clergy penitent privilege, clergy mandated reporting, and First Amendment rights. Religions have argued that they are excluded from reporting accusation of child molestation to the authorities. Since California courts have rulings against these arguments, we are seeking a way to codify those rulings into California law. The intent is to limit the endless litigation.

We have found people working in the California State Capitol to be very helpful. When the issue is explained to staff members, their humanity comes to the fore. They are mothers, fathers, brothers, and sisters. Their instincts to protect family members kick in and many have offered assistance. One mother said her children are precious, and would not want to see them harmed. She added, "I cannot believe the victimization of these people." Those kinds of reactions encourage me to continue, realizing that most people are unaware of the wrongs being done.

I have attached a prospectus for an international SCAARS and hope it will give you an idea of what Robert, Karin, Barbara, Richard and Mark are dreaming about. What do you think? Are you interested in helping us create a larger initiative to protect children from abuse? If so, contact me at: Scaars.ca@gmail.com

If there is enough interest and an adequate number of resourceful volunteers, as well as supporters, we would like to propose that the following new organization and website be created:

A Prospectus

For a Potential New Organization & Related Website

Stop Child Abuse - Advocates for Reform and Safety
scaars.org, scaars.com and scaars.net

The MISSION under consideration for SCAARS is:

1) Increase awareness of *CHILD ABUSE** and the *undue influence* used by groups/people who persuade victims and families of victims to place religious or organizational authority above civil authority;

2) Provide victims of abuse the necessary tools and resources to obtain personal counseling and legal assistance, in order to help them recover;

3) Provide documentation and resources for attorneys and professionals representing victims of child sexual abuse; solicit for a team of qualified attorneys to help write laws;

4) Advocate for legal reform, be it SOL**, mandatory reporting laws or non-disclosure agreements on a state, federal and international level.

5) Change our culture's view of tolerating institutions that use undue influence and First Amendment rights to cover up child sexual abuse, in order to maintain their public image.

*CHILD ABUSE: Physical, Sexual, Mental, Emotional and Spiritual/Religious (Anything causing trauma)
**SOL= Statute of Limitations

83

Potential Objectives being considered for SCAARS are:

1) Develop a child abuse (sexual-abuse focus) web site, which will be a permanent resource in the public domain.

2) Write and publish articles about child abuse related issues, including the latest legislations and outcomes of criminal and civil cases.

3) Provide and maintain a toll-free phone number, to be monitored by professionals, and used for communication with victims, attorneys, etc. ($300 a month) We will advertise anonymous support along with this toll-free number on our website. We will need people like Lee Marsh, who could command such a call center.

4) Welcome victims who have suffered abuse within the Jehovah's Witness and other organizations and provide them a list of professional resources, including counselors who can provide local or online assistance. Include a process for moving from victim, to survivor, to a thriver. Share the opportunity to become a SCAARS advocate/supporter as an expression of recovery.

5) Work with advocates for child abuse tax reform, which will hold organizations responsible for failing to maintain the legal standard of care for members who fall under their jurisdiction.

6) Provide outreach and materials to police, other law enforcement and child protection agents to facilitate awareness of policies/procedures of organizations in which children are at risk.

7) Build a social media presence to accompany the web site. We will use FB and our web forum to create a support mechanism where victims can connect with others, tell their stories, or get connected with the help they need.

8) Provide assistance to filmmakers who are producing documentaries, specifically when they deal with child abuse/molestation matters and abuse reporting procedures.

9) Work with attorneys to help victims of child abuse, and provide research for the law firms supporting victims.

10) Network with other organizations with similar goals, sharing information and resources. Example: Reclaimed Voices at reclaimedvoices.org/, SNAP, abolishsexabuse.org/, and law enforcement agencies.

11) Share/create videos and learning tools on our website to educate children, parents and educators on how to recognize child abuse and report it to civil authorities.

12) Work with legislators to create and enact new laws that will provide better protection for children from pedophiles.

Potential Projects being considered are:

1) Draft a report about Jehovah's Witnesses to government officials, law officers, therapists, child protection authorities, social workers, lawyers, etc.

2) Put together a plan on *how to grow a grass roots movement to change laws.*

3) Articulate how recovering from leaving a religion could include participating in politics as a therapy for some people.

Potential To Do's being considered are:

1) Hire someone to be our webmaster, research analyst and senior editor

2) Design a logo and draft a one-year plan with measurable objectives

3) Appoint an executive review board for SCAARS

Significant Help from my Friends

Richard and I could not have written this book without the support of several very special and talented people. While their contributions appear in several parts of the book, I thought that you might enjoy getting to know all about these caring people. So I have provided the following information about who they are and why helping to write and publish this book was important to them:

Information about Bonnie Zieman

Bonnie was born and raised in the Jehovah's Witness cult. She was a full-time recruiter for that organization and married a JW elder. After the birth of her first child, Bonnie decided to leave that repressive group. She has been ostracized by her family of origin for so doing.

Once out of that education-phobic cult, Bonnie earned a master's degree in education and trained in Gestalt, Psychosynthesis and EMDR therapies. She worked in private practice for over twenty years as a licensed psychotherapist in Montreal, Canada, helping clients come to terms with the existential realities of their lives and recover from various forms of trauma.

Bonnie has written extensively on the subject of recovery after leaving high-control groups, authoring six books related to healing from undue influence and psychological abuse.

- *Shunned: A Survival Guide*
- *Cracking the Cult Code for Therapists: What Every Cult Victim Wants Their Therapist to Know*
- *The Challenge to Heal After Leaving a High-Control Group*
- *The Challenge to Heal Workbook & Journal*
- *Exiting the JW Cult: A Healing Handbook*
- *Fading OUT of the JW Cult: A Memoir*

WHY SHE WANTED TO CONTRIBUTE TO THIS BOOK in Bonnie's words:

I have watched Barbara Anderson's activism against Watchtower deceptions and her advocacy for victims of child sexual abuse in that organization for several years. Having admired her work from a distance, I was excited to be invited to contribute to this book with commentary about the mind-control the JW.ORG exercises over its members, and how intelligent, savvy people can be influenced by their persuasions and controlled by their many forms of threats–implicit and explicit. It has been a privilege to bring my personal experience as a thirty year member of that cult, my twenty plus years of professional experience as a psychotherapist, and my research and work as a writer to this *"Barbara Anderson Uncensored"* project.

May this book alert governments around the globe to Barbara Anderson's impressive body of work documenting JW.ORG abuses, and exposing how children in that cult are easy prey for pedophiles in their midst due to JW.ORG's flagrant failure to provide any duty of care for its most vulnerable members.

Information about Jon Atack

Jon is a writer and scholar on manipulation and undue influence. In 1990, his best-selling history of Scientology, *Let's Sell These People a Piece of Blue Sky* was published. He has helped about 600 people recover from abuse in high-control groups. He is recognized as an expert witness by the English High Court and has been consulted in more than 150 court cases around the world.

Jon was the president of FACTNet (the Fight Against Coercive Tactics Network). He is a founding member of the Open Minds Foundation, a US non-profit organization with outposts in England and Holland. He is the head of the Review Board at the foundation.

Jon has lectured around the world and contributed to many books, articles and media pieces. In the mid-1990s, understanding that the same dynamics apply in all coercive relationships, he shifted his focus to the broad range of groups and individuals using manipulation. He has studied terrorist radicalization, gang formation, and more recently human trafficking, pedophile grooming and coercive control in personal relationships. Jon's book *Opening Minds: the Secret World of Manipulation, Brainwashing and Undue Influence* details his research in these areas.

Jon's publications include: *A Piece of Blue Sky: Scientology, Dianetics and L. Ron Hubbard Exposed*, 1990 (2nd expanded edition, *Let's Sell These People a Piece of Blue Sky*, 2013, 2018); *Scientology: the Cult of Greed*, 2014; *Opening Minds: the Secret World of Manipulation, Brainwashing and Undue Influence*, 2015, revised edition 2018; *A Way to Life, the Tao Te Ching of Lao Tze*, translation 2017

Information about Mariuca Rofick

Mariuca is an artist, a former Jehovah's Witness and married to a Detroit artist Carl Wilson. Her story of discovery and of nurturing her authentic identity is an inspirational read in *Mariuca & Marilyn, Saying Good-Bye to Mama's Club*.

Information about Lee Elder

Lee Elder is the founder and current acting director of AJWRB (Advocates for Jehovah's Witness Reform on Blood). Lee Elder is a pseudonym that he began using while still an active Jehovah's Witness elder in the mid 1990's. This allowed him to maintain his status as a JW, and begin an organized effort from within the Watchtower organization to reform the blood policy.

Lee is no longer active as a JW, but continues to advocate on behalf of JWs, and educate both patients and the medical community about the many irrational aspects of Watchtower's blood policy. It is his hope that one day all JW members will have the opportunity to make fully informed choices regarding their healthcare, free from Watchtower's mandated extreme shunning and undue influence.

Information about Frances Peters

Frances Peters is a *Certified Academic Coach/Counselor* at FreeChoice in the Netherlands. She was born into the Jehovah's Witness religion, and left that organization in 2004 with her husband and their two children. Frances has helped many former members to reclaim their lives.

Frances has written several magazine articles about the influence of cult behavior on identity development and the dark side of religion, as well as lecturing on the topic. Since 2011 she has co-hosted a support group for former members of cults, abusive groups and relationships – OwnFreeChoice Praatcafé. She is also the spokesperson for Open Minds Foundation in the Netherlands.

Information about Joanna Foreman

Joanna Foreman has a long writing career, spanning over two decades. The five senses of taste, touch, smell, sight, and sound play notable roles in her stories. In her memoir and its follow-up, *The Know-it-all Girl Grows Up,* she portrays herself waltzing through the hoops of her mother's religion as a Jehovah's Witness, which she recognized as a cult only after she'd escaped from it.

While writing her latest novel, *Riverwalk Chameleon,* she made numerous trips to San Antonio, memorizing the Riverwalk's unique sounds, scenery, and aromas to stimulate her muse for continued writing. The sixth sense plays a major role in her short fiction collection, *Ghostly Hauntings of Interstate-65.* She has benefitted from membership, and has contributed stories to The Southern Indiana Writers Group's annual anthologies since 2006.

Joanna learned early on the value of all five senses as she created her storybook life. During childhood, she cherished summer weekends in a two-room cabin with her family, a mere 20 feet from the banks of Brandywine Creek in Shelby County, Indiana. Musical echoes of nature accompanied her barefoot treks through tall grasses to select ripe raspberries in the wild; nighttime campfires offered warmth and wood-scented grilled delicacies.

She once lived so close to the Indianapolis Speedway she heard the squeal of tires zipping around the racetrack throughout the Indy 500. At one point, she lived a mile from Louisville's Churchill Downs where she heard the famous Kentucky Derby bugle call.

Joanna and her husband Craig stood barefoot on St. Augustine Beach as they married in 2001. They reside in a rustic home with their English Setter, in the middle of two wooded acres, having put down roots "back home again" in Indiana, where they plan to live happily ever after.

Information about Mark J. O'Donnell

Mark O'Donnell, a native of Baltimore Maryland, is a researcher, writer, and advocate for child protection and the elimination of undue influence.

Born in 1967, Mark was raised as a devout Jehovah's Witness. Baptized in 1984, he was raised to believe the end of the world was imminent. Education was useless in light of Armageddon. He was isolated from society, only sharing friendships with fellow believers with no ambition and no education. Their only hope was the dangling carrot of a future utopian world, called the "new system."

Actively involved in JW activities, Mark spent 10 years as a Ministerial Servant. In lieu of an education, he started a successful small business and traveled the world, visiting fellow JWs and branch facilities in Europe, Asia, the Americas, Australia and the South Pacific. He was an integral part of Kingdom Hall Construction in Maryland, as well as hurricane relief work in the Caribbean Islands.

Married in 1998 to Kimberly, a fellow JW, Mark and his wife

expected to live out their lives as loyal members of their faith. That came to an end in early 2014, when Mark walked away from the organization, never to return.

Following his conscience, Mark realized that the JW religion had taken the best years of his life and filled them with false hope, and supplied an endless stream of conditional friendships, which vanished when he stopped attending meetings.

After his exit from the JWs, he discovered the massive child abuse cover-up within the organization and a multitude of deceptions and false teachings. Mark's research abilities and in-depth knowledge of the organization presented him the opportunity to write for numerous websites, including AvoidJW.org and JW-survey.org.

Today, Mark works with journalists, law enforcement officers, therapists, attorneys and advocates for reform in an effort to create transparency, and force groups like JWs to abandon their practices which destroy families, friendships, and lives. His research focuses on the increasing numbers of JW child abuse cases worldwide, as well as the issue of organizational influence over personal medical decisions.

Mark was invited to speak at the Reveal Conference in London in April 2017, sponsored by the Center for Investigative Reporting. He has been interviewed by many journalists, and lends his research to media professionals around the world.

Mark continues to report on the activities of JWs and is currently working on several documentaries about the group. He is also a supporter of the Open Minds Foundation, which is a global initiative aimed at promoting freedom of mind.

Information about Lee Marsh

Lee Marsh was introduced to Jehovah's Witnesses when she was 11 years old, and she was baptized at age 17. She married a recent JW convert and they parented two children. Her husband eventually became an elder. Lee left the JWs when she was 35 and enrolled at a university in Montreal, Canada.

After graduation, Lee established the first resource center for adult survivors of sexual abuse (Centre for Incest Healing) and for 13 years worked with over 600 men and women. After that she worked in a homeless shelter with survivors of various forms of abuse and later worked with battered women.

Over the last 18 years she has spent countless hours online to help survivors of sexual abuse and domestic violence after they leave Watchtower. She has also offered support and information to those who have left the Witnesses and been subsequently shunned by their Witness family members and friends.

Lee is the president for Advocates for Awareness of Watchtower Abuses (aawa.co) and an advisor to the board of the Open Minds Foundation (openminds.org) and lives in Ottawa, Canada.

Information about Mike White

Mike and his wife, Tama, own http://www.ghostriverimages.com/. For more than 25 years they have helped writers tell and publish their stories. They build books for authors and organizations and consult and teach on all matters related to publishing. If you like what you see and read, thank Mike. Richard and I could not have told you my story without his help.

Information about Carl Wilson

Carl, www.carlwilson.com, is a Detroit artist influenced by expressionist print makers. He kindly helped with the graphic design cover for this book.

Information about Richard E. "Dick" Kelly

Richard is a Trustee and the Secretary-Treasurer for the Open Minds Foundation https://www.openmindsfoundation.org/. He manages Advocates for Awareness of Watchtower Abuses http://aawa.co/, and he has written three books: *Growing Up in Mama's Club – A Childhood Perspective of Jehovah's Witnesses*, *The Ghost of Mama's Club*, and *Mariuca & Marilyn: Saying Good-bye to Mama's Club*.

Richard was born in 1943 and spent most of his childhood in Los Angeles, California. When he was four years of age, his parents became Jehovah's Witnesses (the Club), and firm believers that the end of the world would occur before he reached the age of twenty. To ensure his survival at Armageddon, he had to attend five one-hour meetings a week at a Kingdom Hall and travel to three conventions a year. He was also required to spend at least twelve hours a month in the door-to-door work selling the Watchtower and other Club literature.

Dick wasn't allowed to participate in Little League or high school sports. And he was not permitted to attend college. In 1958, in response to a special calling from the Club "to serve where the need was great," his family moved to a small town in eastern Nebraska. After graduating from high school, Dick became a "pioneer", spending 100 hours a month in the door-to-door work for over a year. In 1962 he volunteered to live and work at Bethel, the Club's headquarters, in Brooklyn, NY.

After two years at Bethel, Dick turned in his resignation and ended his association with the Club. Dick was married in 1964 and he and his wife, Helen, lived in New York City for a year. They moved to western Michigan in 1965, where they raised a son and daughter. Dick has an accounting degree and MBA, and he worked 33 years for Clipper Belt Lacer Company, a Grand Rapids manufacturer. He served as treasurer for ten years and president for seventeen years.

Dick retired in 1997. A year later his youngest sister, Marilyn, was brutally stabbed to death. Dick's mama was given power of attorney for her remains, and since Marilyn had left the Club three years before, no memorial service was held. As far as Mama and other Jehovah's Witnesses were concerned, because she wasn't one of them, Marilyn was dead and forgotten. Dick brooded for several months before deciding to write his story about growing up in Mama's Club, knowing the damage that is done when children, particularly his sister, are forced to adhere to religious ideology they were not intellectually or emotionally able to comprehend.

Barbara Has More to Say

BARBARA ANDERSON
UNCENSORED

When a JW minor is sexually abused by a fellow member of the congregation, typically the elders are informed and then an investigation ensues. Instructions from JW leaders in place since 1989, require that two elders immediately call the Legal Department of that country's JW branch office for legal advice and then elders are to start an investigation.

Before JW leaders sent instructions in a letter dated August 1, 2016 to all elders mandating that "a victim of child sexual abuse is not required to make an allegation in the presence of the alleged abuser" during a judicial committee process, most elders did indeed demand this of the victim believing they were following a biblical injunction. Furthermore, enduring intimate questioning by three males was a secondary violation and terrifying for a victim who wasn't permitted to even have an advocate in the room.

Children were terrorized by sexual abuse and then they were re-abused having to try to present their case in a room of male authority figures. In many, if not in most cases, child victims were discounted, implicitly shamed, and received little or no help or supportive direction. As damaging as that was, consulting a mental-health professional was discouraged.

For over six decades this was the situation that confronted JW victims of child sexual abuse. The elders in these scenarios were so uninformed and so ill-equipped to handle such situations that they were unaware of the harm they did to an already suffering minor or adult who finally had the courage to come forward with an accusation. Only since recent public outcry have Jehovah's Witnesses leaders allowed other changes, such as elders reporting sexual abuse to the authorities without sanctions; treating victims supportively and with compassion, and permitting victims to seek help through therapy.

However, because the JWs continue to use an ancient Bible rule to discipline members that require two witnesses to wrongdoing to corroborate an accusation, a molester is rarely reported to the authorities if there is not an eye-witness; especially, if there isn't a clergy-mandated reporting law in the state where the crime occurred.

Another rule that protects the molester and puts kids in danger is after guilt of the accused was not established by another witness, the accuser is not permitted to discuss the allegation with others because this may well damage the reputation of the accused. In these circumstances, confidentiality for the one blamed is maintained and sexual predators use this to their advantage to groom other children. – Per Barbara Anderson

Jehovah's Witnesses Recent U.S. Child Abuse Policies and Procedures are Inadequate

The September 1, 2017 letter TO ALL BODIES OF ELDERS, Re: Protecting Minors From Abuse, was sent by the Christian Congregation of Jehovah's Witnesses (CCJW), a religious corporation chartered by the State of New York, and not from the WATCHTOWER BIBLE AND TRACT SOCIETY OF NEW YORK, INC. as formerly.

Basically, this six-page letter consisting of twenty-seven paragraphs, updating previous rules, regulations, procedures, and policies was issued to Jehovah's Witnesses (JW's) elders to supposedly protect minors from abuse. The letter is insistent that it is the responsibility of the parents to protect their children. If this is the case, then why put this obligation upon the elders? However, upon close examination, it's obvious the majority of the rules protects the religious corporation, CCJW, from liability in the case of a civil lawsuit, and do not protect children from molestation.

The entire letter is in accordance with "The LAW" and is certainly not about right and wrong. After all, it was prepared by in-house attorneys located at JW's World Headquarters in upstate New York, probably with input from the best outside legal counsel money could buy.

However, to the average individual when scanning the letter's instructions, the "optics" doesn't look quite right. Particularly when the instructions require anyone who reports an allegation of abuse to the elders is to be informed that they have the right to report the matter to the secular authorities. That's an improvement from the past, but everyone knows an accuser has the right to report abuse, but nowhere in the letter is there a statement to elders to strongly press for the accuser to call the authorities immediately, although virtually every adult other than JWs believe that the authorities should be called first if child sex crimes are suspected. Not making this demand is "undue influence" by giving accusers a choice where there should be no choice respecting molestation reporting.

Other examples of instructions that are not illegal, but certainly imprudent, are directives to elders to 'investigate' all allegations of child abuse even though they have no training whatsoever; setting layers of bureaucracy (rules and regulations) between the victim, perpetrator and the law; elders deciding who is "guilty" of abuse based on an archaic Bible-based belief of the JW's that "two witnesses" are needed to determine guilt, which a one-time director of the Survivors Network of those Abused by Priests (SNAP) observed is, "a stunningly heartless and reckless policy that is guaranteed to cause more heinous crimes against children."

Rather than trained experts defining what abuse is, untrained elders define abuse based on instructions from JWs leaders in New York. They also follow NY's instructions when a man claims repentance after molesting a child whether he can be used in a ministerial position in the congregation "if ever" or "rarely."

The letter states in paragraph three: "The congregation's handling of an accusation of child sexual abuse is not intended to replace the secular authority's handling of the matter." If this is really the case, why does the letter contain instructions on how three elders should investigate child abuse allegations? Why are instructions given about convening judicial hearings? Why are instructions from headquarters for elders needed so they can pronounce guilt or innocence on an accused member? Paragraph five – Legal Considerations, in the letter even states: "Child abuse is a crime." If this is so, why are elders investigating this crime? That's the authorities' domain.

If JW's leaders would instruct elders to report abuse as soon as possible and let the experts do their job, all of the above rules wouldn't be necessary. That's what most other religions do nowadays with few legal problems for the religious organization.

Twenty-seven paragraphs of policies to protect a child from abuse certainly would be welcomed by the members, not twenty-seven rules in five-paragraphs that are solely concerned with Legal Considerations!

All policies in this letter coming from JW's religious corporation that calls itself a Bible-based organization are not illegal in the U.S. but, to my mind, senseless, when one phone call to the authorities would be consistent with reality and protect all concerned by law.

Jehovah's Witnesses' Child Sex Abuse Cases Bring Religion's Practices Into Question

Christian Post
By Sami K. Martin, Christian Post Reporter October 8, 2014
The Jehovah's Witnesses have a silent epidemic of child abuse that was recently brought to public attention again after four alleged victims filed lawsuits against the organization.

There are over 7 million Jehovah's Witnesses across the

globe, according to the group's website. However, there have been numerous accusations and cases brought against elders and leaders of the organization, alleging child abuse of both young men and women, dating back at least 30 years. Four reported victims brought a lawsuit against the Jehovah's Witnesses and Watchtower Organization in Connecticut.

"This is an insidious problem, an epidemic problem with child sex abuse within this organization that so far seems more concerned about protecting its reputation from scandal than about the children," attorney Irwin Zalkin said at a press conference in Connecticut.

One particular case in 2012 saw Candace Conti, a victim, receive awarded $28 million in damages after alleging that member Jonathan Kendrick molested her from 1995-1996. The case was filed in Oakley, California and the $28 million award was the largest paid to a single victim.

"Nothing can bring back my childhood. But through this (verdict) and through, hopefully, a change in their policy, we can make something good come out of it," Conti said at the time.

Jim McCabe, the attorney who represented the religious organization in the case, said that the Jehovah's Witnesses "hate child abuse and believe it's a plague on humanity. Jonathan Kendrick was not a leader or a pastor; he was just a rank-and-file member. This is a tragic case where a member of a religious group has brought liability on the group for actions he alone may have taken."

The Jehovah's Witnesses have plenty of information on their website about how to keep children safe from predators, but take a unique approach to dealing with cases of accused abuse. When an allegation against a member or elder is made, the organization follows a "two-witness rule," which requires that there be two victims made. They claim that they follow Biblical principles when it comes to the rule and cite Scripture such as 1 Timothy 5:19 and Deuteronomy 19:15, which speak of having two persons come forward when making an accusation.

"You can disagree with our religion all you like, but we are a Bible-based organization, and we stand for upholding the Bible. What we are doing is simply being consistent with the Bible laws and principles, and as much as you dislike the outcome, we have told everyone of our stand, and you can't fault us for being consistent," the organization said in its defense of the rule.

In 2013, Elder Ronald Lawrence was charged with 19 felony counts: 11 of lewd molestation, seven of forcible sodomy and one of rape by instrumentation. The victims included two females and one male in Pittsburgh.

"He admitted to his church that all of the allegations were true" to be re-instated in his church after being "disfellowshipped" by the congregation to which he belonged, the affidavit read. However, Lawrence said that he never admitted anything and denied committing any crimes.

"The actions of the church, their banishment of (Lawrence) on one or more occasion and the directives of the governing body toward the victims and their family members regarding these crimes were actions of 'concealment' and further actions preventing the victims from reporting the crimes to law enforcement," the motion filed in Pittsburgh County District Court read.

The case against Lawrence was dropped in March 2014 due to an objection by the state. However, the prosecutor in the case plans to appeal the decision.

A call was placed to the Jehovah's Witnesses organization in Brooklyn, New York, to discuss the matter further, but no comment was given.

http://www.christianpost.com/news/jehovahs-witnesses-child-sex-abuse-cases-bring-religions-practices-into-question-127738/

Children Are Harmed by Bible-Based Belief

In a recent article, "JW's Child Sex Abuse Cases Bring Religion's Practices Into Question," Sami K. Martin, Christian Post Reporter, frequently uses the word "rule" when explaining JWs demand for two witnesses in cases of child abuse:

"The Jehovah's Witnesses have plenty of information on their website about how to keep children safe from predators, but take a unique approach to dealing with cases of accused abuse. When an allegation against a member or elder is made, the organization follows a "two-witness rule," which requires that there be two victims made. They claim that they follow Biblical principles when it comes to the rule and cite Scripture, such as 1 Timothy 5:19 and Deuteronomy 19:15, which speak of having two persons come forward when making an accusation."

Following that explanation, the reporter quotes Watchtower attorney, Jim McCabe, where McCabe points to the Bible, and not to a mere human organizational rule, as the basis for the religion's requirement of two witnesses to an accusation of child abuse by saying,

"What we are doing is simply being consistent with the Bible laws and principles, and as much as you dislike the outcome, we have told everyone of our stand, and you can't fault us for being consistent," the organization said in its defense of the rule."

Note, McCabe referred to the subject under discussion–a need for two witnesses–as "being consistent" with "Bible laws." By prefacing the words "laws" and also "principles" with the word "Bible," McCabe directed the reader's attention not to easily-altered, man-made organizational laws, but to laws of God which have to be obeyed whether they were uttered 3,500 years ago as Deuteronomy 19:15 was or 2,000 years ago as 1 Timothy 5:19.

It's obvious from Attorney McCabe's statement, this religious organization knows full-well what the outcome of its Bible-based two-witness law and principle is, and no matter how horrible the results are, the organization is not going to change its religious stance just because "...you dislike the outcome."

McCabe's words were insensitive, unsympathetic and irresponsible. He could just as well have said, "We just don't care what you think, and don't care what the outcome of our Bible-based belief is even if it means more molestation, more damage, more injury, more maltreatment, or more crime committed by Jehovah's Witnesses to their brothers in the faith, our two-witness belief remains the same. We will not abandon the two-witness mandate because it's one of the cornerstone Biblical BELIEFS of our religion."

David Clohessy, former executive director of the Survivors Network of those Abused by Priests (SNAP), the world's oldest and largest support group for clergy abuse victims, made the following statement in a press release that nails this Bible-based belief of the Witnesses:

"Outside of the Jehovah's Witness hierarchy, virtually every other adult believes that we should all call police if we see or suspect child sex crimes. ... But the JW hierarchy is wrong on both fronts–policy and performance, belief and behavior...The "two witnesses" rule is a stunningly heartless and reckless policy that is guaranteed to cause more heinous crimes against children."

There are so many other projects, articles, and initiatives that I would love to share with you, but unfortunately the design of this book does not permit. To learn more about these, please visit my website at http://watchtowerdocuments.org/document-library/ One article in particular, Flawed Decree Conceals Criminals, is something you may find very interesting.

The article discusses new discoveries about a JW policy instructing JWs to report a fellow JW, who commits a serious wrongdoing/crime to church elders, even if it was illegal in certain circumstances to do so. The article identifies the Governing Body member who originated the policy and much more.

Barbara Anderson in the News: 2001 – 2018

http://watchtowerdocuments.org/barbara-andersons-profile/

Barbara Anderson is an unstoppable advocate for child protection and outspoken critic of the Watchtower Bible & Tract Society's doctrines that "unduly influence" Jehovah's Witnesses and protects sexual predators. She is an expert on the Watchtower's history. She has been interviewed on major TV and radio programs because of her extensive research on child sexual abuse.

As an advocate for child protection, Barbara aids lawyers suing the Watchtower about child sexual abuse and media investigative journalists as an expert on the cover-up by the Watchtower of child sexual abuse by Jehovah's Witnesses molesters.

Summary of Accomplishments

* Researched child sexual abuse by Witnesses for the Watchtower's Governing Body.
* Owner of www.watchtowerdocuments.org.
* Interviewed on major TV and radio programs about the Watchtower's policies and litigation.

MEDIA: 40 or more reports or interviews regarding Barbara Anderson's activities - 2001 through 2018

- 2001 - Spoke at an ICSA Conference in Orlando, Florida
- Nineteen (19) newspapers, including the New York Times, reported during 2001-2002 Barbara Anderson's public stand against Watchtower's child abuse policies.
- Interviewed on NBC's "Dateline" which aired on May 28, 2002, regarding the Watchtower's child sexual abuse problems. https://vimeo.com/160789542
- Barbara and Joe Anderson interviewed on WKRN-TV News 2, at 6 PM on September 5, 2002. Also appeared twice on WSMV–TV News 4, September 5, 2002, first at 5 PM and at 6 PM. https://youtu.be/seUMzyekbJI
- Radio interview on the Mark Furhman Show, Spokane, WA, October 17, 2005.
- Appeared in an expose' about secret out-of-court settlements by the Watchtower on NBC Nightly News with Brian Williams that aired November 21, 2007. https://www.youtube.com/watch?v=N9Xjw_sk7tA and WSMV, Nashville, TN –https://www.youtube.com/watch?v=JDzz8waKlnI
- Assisted attorneys in lawsuits and the media to better understand the Watchtower's policies and Witness mindsets. http://watchtowerdocuments.org/zalkin-court-case-documents/; http://watchtowerdocuments.org/candace-conti-court-documents/ and http://watchtowerdocuments.org/free-downloadable-files/secrets-of-pedophilia-in-an-american-religion/
- Produced the "Secrets" CD describing the secret out-of-court settlements by the Watchtower. http://watchtowerdocuments.org/free-downloadable-files/
- European tour of five countries in 2009 speaking at the Vatican and two major Catholic churches about JWs and child abuse.
- 2009 - Also spoke at the University of Geneva and gave two lectures in Paris sponsored by a French Governmental agency, MILIVUDES.
- 2009 - In connection with MILIVUDES, Barbara had a private interview with an undersecretary of the then French presi-

dent regarding JWs and their cover-up of child abuse. http://watchtowerdocuments.org/opening-pandoras-box-speech/; http://www.testimoni-di-geova.info/spip.php?article19; http://ilmondocristiano.myblog.it/2010/04/17/barbara-anderson-atto-d-accusa-contro-i-testimoni-di-geova/

- "Growing Up With Jehovah," a Swiss TV documentary that aired in French starting in November, 2010 with the Andersons discussing child abuse (copyright video in French language available on site) The documentary aired in many French-speaking countries since 2010. http://www.rts.ch/emissions/temps-present/2482487-grandir-avec-jehovah.html
- Cult Free Radio – Mad Sweeney interviewing Barbara Anderson, broadcast October 15, 2011 Part one – https://www.youtube.com/watch?v=9NYd9U3KfrU; Part two – https://www.youtube.com/watch?v=oMmlqbwEkVM&t=70s
- Radio interview November 11, 2014, on the Chuck Morse Show-Boston, MA https://www.youtube.com/watch?v=-800BSEqvL0
- Appeared on an Investigation Discovery program August 3, 2015 in the Robert and Janet Bryant story. http://watchtowerdocuments.org/barbara-on-investigation-discovery-channel-id-in-august-2015/#more-6790. The following link is for a short ID program about the damage of shunning taken from Barbara's interview with an ID producer.
- http://www.investigationdiscovery.com/deadly-devotion-fallback/the-psychological-toll-shunning-takes-on-peoples-lives/
- Appeared in Quebec, Canada, French documentary that aired on CBC, December 1, 2016: "The Kingdom's Dirty Secrets" – Documentary in ENGLISH on Barbara's website with her personal introduction:http://watchtowerdocuments.org/canadian-documentary-exposes-watchtowers-dirty-secrets/#more-8404 or on YouTube: https://www.youtube.com/watch?v=_AJPHGMt9JI
- October 14, 2017, spoke at the International Cultic Studies Association Conference on the subject of Spiritual Abuse at Middle Tennessee State University, Murfreesboro, Tennessee.

Other Media Links found at http:// watchtowerdocuments.org/media-room/

Child sex-abuse activist Anderson interviewed on national TV show on church allegations – Tullahoma News and Guardian – 2007

UNADFI – French anti-cult organization covers Barbara's 2009 European Tour

Woman Says Church Covering Up Sexual Abuse – WSMV Nashville – 2008

New Evidence in Jehovah's Witnesses Allegations – MSNBC – 2007

Jehovah's Witnesses Settle Abuse Cases – Associated Press – 2007

21 Newspaper articles 2001 - 2002

Tri-City Herald (Washington State) News - August 16th 2001:
Thursday-August 16, 2001
By Shirley Wentworth

http://pages.globetrotter.net/mleblank/org/pedopointdevuea.html
- August 25th 2001:
JW Child Abuse: An Insider's Insight
By Barbara Anderson

The Courier-Journal Newspaper - May 8th 2002:
Jehovah's Witnesses act against abuse-policy critics
By Peter Smith, psmith@courier-journal.com

CNN News Website - May 9th 2002:
Four Jehovah's Witnesses fight church's handling of child abuse cases

KUALA LUMPUR, Malaysia News - May 9, 2002   http://
library.northernlight.com/EC20020509450000047.
html?cb=0&dx=1006&sc=0#doc
Jehovah's Witnesses say they may be ousted over sex abuse
comments

New York Post Newspaper - May 9th 2002:
FOUR FACING JEHOVAH OUSTER
By DAN MANGAN

NEW YORK TIMES Newspaper - May 9th 2002:
National Briefing: Religion
By Laurie Goodstein (NYT)

TORONTO STAR Newspaper - May 10th 2002:
Sex scandal hits church
Four Jehovah's Witnesses face ouster for protest

The Tullahoma News - May 11th 2002:
Whistleblower could lose her church, family
MARY REEVES, Special to The News

The Tennessean Newspaper - May 11th 2002:
Abuse charges put Witness at risk of shunning
Barbara Anderson, of the Manchester Congregation of Jehovah's
Witnesses, faces possible disciplinary action.
By LEON ALLIGOOD and EMILY HEFFTER and Staff Writers

WashingtonPost.com News - May 11th 2002:
In Brief - Saturday, Page B08
Ouster Looms for Critics Of Sex Abuse Policy

The Tennessean Newspaper - May 16th 2002:
Jehovah's Witnesses downplay sex abuse, women say
By LEON ALLIGOOD, Staff Writer

NEW YORK TIMES - August 11th 2002 Edition:
Ousted Members Contend Jehovah's Witnesses' Abuse Policy
Hides Offenses
By LAURIE GOODSTEIN

"Toasted Cheese" E-Zine Story - September 3rd 2002:
An Unlikely David: Barbara Anderson's struggle to stop preda-
tory pedophiles in the cloistered world of Jehovah's Witnesses
By Michael Morris (Mike Pence)

"Dances With Cactus" Web Blog on Salon.com - September 4th
2002:
Wednesday
How Many More?
By Michael Morris (Mike Pence)

WSMV Nashville, Tennessee NBC Affiliate News Channel 4 -
September 5th 2002:
Former church members march in protest
People say they were molested as a child by a Jehovah's Witness
By James Lewis

WKRN Nashville, Tennessee News Channel 2 - September 5th
2002:
Sexual Abuse Allegations Within Jehovah's Witness Denomination
Reporter: Wisdom Martinaaaa

Tennessean.com News - September 6th 2002:
Couple to protest Jehovah's Witnesses
By LEON ALLIGOOD, Staff Writer

The Tullahoma News and Guardian (Tennessee) Newspaper --
Wednesday, September 11th 2002:
http://www.tullahomanews.com
Couple plans to march against church denomination's policy
By BRIAN JUSTICE, Staff Writer September 11, 2002

Associated Press (AP) News Story - September 26th 2002
(This story was in many different newspapers!)
Ex-Jehovah's Witnesses Speak Out
Thursday September 26, 2002

The Tullahoma News – November 09, 2002
Banned church member sues Jehovah's Witnesses
By BRIAN JUSTICE, The Sunday News Staff Writer

Miscellaneous Documents Related to Child Abuse

In this section of the book I have included a variety of links and information about child sexual abuse, which you may find of interest.

The following link is to a 11-21-2007 website news release from NBC's Nightly News with Brian Williams:
http://www.nbcnews.com/id/21917798/page/2/#.Wo7eOIPwYdV
or
http://www.nbcnews.com/id/21917798/page/2/#.Wo4HROly7L8

In part: "However, NBC News has obtained a copy of one of the settlements from the McLean lawsuit, and it may offer an indication of the potential magnitude of the payouts. According to the court record, the church agreed to pay $781,250 to the accuser, who claimed McLean abused her from age 3 to age 9. (After legal fees and other costs, the accuser was set to receive approximately $530,000.)"

The following link is to articles that will help you better understand the effects of child sexual abuse:
https://www.secasa.com.au/pages/how-children-cope-with-the-pain-of-sexual-assault/

Simply stated, to survive a child has to develop psychological defense mechanisms. These defense mechanisms help them survive during the abuse, and in maintaining a balance between feeling and expressing stored pain and continuing to function in daily life. The three major defenses commonly used are: Memory suppression, dissociation and denial.
https://www.healthyplace.com/abuse/child-sexual-abuse/effects-of-child-sexual-abuse-on-children/

This link discusses the many and varied effects of child sexual abuse, as seen in children of any age, as no child is psychologically prepared to cope with sexual stimulation. Even a two or three year old, who cannot know the sexual activity is wrong will develop problems resulting from the inability to cope with effects of child sexual abuse.

Las Vegas REVIEW-JOURNAL: Las Vegas man charged with raping teen member of his church

https://www.reviewjournal.com/crime/sex-crimes/las-vegas-man-charged-with-raping-teen-member-of-his-church/

By Blake Apgar / Las Vegas Review-Journal

March 23, 2018 - 5:10 pm; Updated March 23, 2018 - 6:32

A Las Vegas man was arrested last week after authorities accused him of raping a teenage member of his church, police and court records show.

Carlos Alfonso Perez, 55, was charged in January with three counts of sexual assault with a minor under 14 and two counts of sexual assault with a minor under 16, records show. He was arrested March 13 at his northeast Las Vegas home. Perez is accused of assaulting a teenage girl multiple times between July 2012 and July 2014. He denied any wrongdoing in a December interview with police, according to records, but declined to take a polygraph examination.

The girl was 13 at the time the abuse began, according to a police report. She and Perez attended the same kingdom hall of Jehovah's Witnesses for more than 10 years, according to the report, and the girl saw him multiple times a week at church functions.

She eventually reported the abuse to church officials, who had her confront Perez face to face, according to the police report.

"The church members decided that there was nothing they could do, since the stories were different," the report states.

The document makes no mention of church officials attempting to contact police. A spokesman for Jehovah's Witnesses in New York did not respond to requests for comment on Thursday and Friday. According to the document, the girl reported Perez to police in August.

Barbara Anderson's analysis of this report:

Note in the article that the assaults on the teenager occurred "between July 2012 and July 2014." The police report stated that "she eventually reported the abuse to church officials, who had her confront Perez face to face."

The procedure of requiring a victim to confront her abuser was common for decades until the letter TO ALL BODIES OF ELDERS, dated August 1, 2016, page 3, par. 13 instructed: "Elders should remember that during the investigation process and during the judicial committee process, a victim of child sexual abuse is not required to make her allegation in the presence of the alleged abuser."

Especially since the early years of the 21st century, JW leadership has been highly criticized for requiring a JW child abuse victim to confront an alleged JW abuser during a meeting with elders present. This procedure regularly occurred because of elders applying the scripture in Matthew 18:15.

For those abused this was a horrible experience that caused many victims to suffer from psychological damage. In Sept. 2002, Victoria Boer, in Canada, sued the Watchtower of Canada because two representatives at Watchtower's Canadian headquarters instructed a local elder to make her confront her molester, her father, in a 1989 meeting in obedience to Matthew 18:15.

COURT FILE NO: 9K-CV-154117
DATE of release of court decision: June 26, 2003
ONTARIO SUPERIOR COURT OF JUSTICE
BETWEEN VICTORIA BOER, Plaintiff
Charles C. Mark for the Plaintiff
AND
BRIAN CAIRNS, STEVE BROWN, JOHN DIDUR, AND
WATCH TOWER BIBLE AND TRACT SOCIETY OF CANADA,
Defendants
Colin P. Stevenson and Maureen L. Whelton for the Defendants
Heard September 9,10,11,12,13,16,17,18,19,20,23, and 24,2002

"INTRODUCTION
The plaintiff Victoria Boer seeks punitive damages and damages
for negligence and breach of fiduciary duty against the Watchtower Bible and Tract Society of Canada (the governing body of
Jehovah's Witnesses in Canada) and three elders of that church.
Her claim stems from actions taken by the Jehovah's Witnesses
elders when, at the age of 19, she disclosed to them that she had
been sexually molested by her father during her childhood. The
plaintiff alleges that she was forced to confront her father with
these allegations in the presence of two male elders of her congregation, an experience which she found to be traumatic. She said
she was then required to go through essentially the same exercise
of confrontation again, this time before three male elders, as part
of a church disciplinary process against her father, thereby com-
pounding the trauma. She further alleges that Watchtower failed
to properly deal with the abuse by her father, failed to report it
as required by law, and directed her not to seek medical and psychological treatment. The plaintiff testified that as a result of the
defendant's wrongdoing she has suffered extreme emotional harm
which was for years untreated and which will require extensive
therapy in the future.

"PART OF THE JUDGES DECISION:
Ms. Boer contacted Mr. Longworth in his capacity as an elder
of the church. Mr. Longworth consulted throughout with more
senior advisers at the Jehovah's Witness head office and passed

on their advice to the plaintiff. He acted at all times as an agent of the defendant Watch Tower. The defendant Watch Tower did not seek to distance itself from the conduct of Longworth and the other elders who provided advice to Ms. Boer in Toronto or to disclaim any responsibility for their actions. Although the statement of claim could be clearer on this point, I believe that on a fair reading of the pleading and subsequently delivered particulars, there is an allegation that Watch Tower is responsible for the harm suffered by the plaintiff as a result of the direction given to her to apply Matthew 18:15-18. Accordingly, I find the defendant Watch Tower Bible and Tract Society of Canada liable to the plaintiff for the harm she sustained as a result of attending the December 29, 1989 meeting."

Joe and I attended the Boer trial. We learned later that after the Boer case, a Canadian law was enacted that specified that it was illegal to force a victim of child abuse to confront their abuser. The question remains as to why did it take so long for JWs Governing Body to put a stop to this terrifying procedure that went on for as many as six decades when a JW victim of crime by a JW member reported it to the elders, as required by JW leadership. This is just one of the bizarre interpretations of scripture that has brought so much suffering to tens of thousands of JWs through the years, which, thankfully, the media is bringing to the attention of the public and law enforcement.

You will find more information about this subject material at http://watchtowerdocuments.org/document-library/

Made in the USA
San Bernardino,
CA

57538462R00064